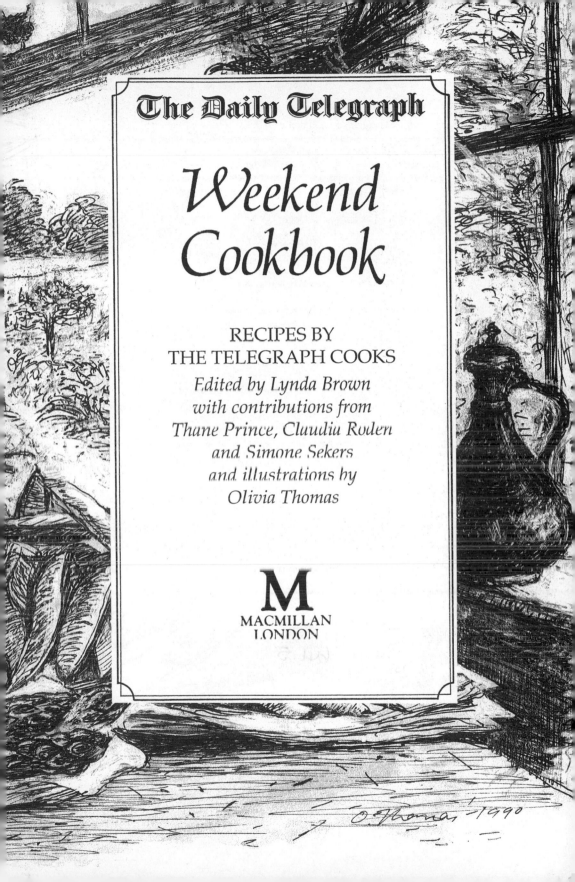

The Daily Telegraph

Weekend Cookbook

RECIPES BY
THE TELEGRAPH COOKS

Edited by Lynda Brown
with contributions from
Thane Prince, Claudia Roden
and Simone Sekers
and illustrations by
Olivia Thomas

M
MACMILLAN
LONDON

First published 1991 by
MACMILLAN LONDON LIMITED
Cavaye Place London SW10 9PG
and Basingstoke

Associated companies in Auckland, Delhi, Dublin, Gaborone, Hamburg,
Harare, Hong Kong, Johannesburg, Kuala Lumpur, Lagos, Manzini, Melbourne,
Mexico City, Nairobi, New York, Singapore and Tokyo

ISBN 0-333-56568-1

A CIP catalogue record for this book is available from the British Library

Typeset by Macmillan Production Limited

Printed by Billing and Sons Limited, Worcester

For Claudia, Simone and Thane

CONTENTS

ACKNOWLEDGEMENTS

I should like to thank, firstly, those publishers who allowed me to reprint recipes previously published elsewhere, in particular BBC Publications, Century Hutchinson and Penguin Books.

To my colleagues Claudia Roden, Thane Prince and Simone Sekers, I give my grateful thanks for their patience and co-operation, and at times much-needed good-humoured understanding.

To my editor, Judith Hannam, I should like to express particular thanks. Her support and gentle fastidiousness throughout has been the lynchpin of this book. And last but by no means least, Trevor Grove, then editor of the Weekend *Daily Telegraph* and now editor of *The Sunday Telegraph*, who first gathered us together and without whom this book could never have borne fruit; and to Marilyn Warnick, who had the vision to make it all happen.

LYNDA BROWN

Introduction

THE WEEKEND COOKBOOK is compiled from recipes which have appeared on the Food and Drink pages of the Weekend section of *The Daily Telegraph* over the last three or four years, written by Weekend contributors Claudia Roden, Thane Prince, Simone Sekers and myself. To make the book as comprehensive as possible, additional recipes have been included here and there, where I felt appropriate. I have also endeavoured to fill in any gaps, and, throughout the book, Simone Sekers has provided lively information and useful hints about ingredients and foodstuffs in general. Though the book contains many hot and cold desserts, cakes and puddings have, by and large, not been included. These are admirably catered for by Thane Prince in her forthcoming book, *Cakes, Bakes and Puddings*, to be published by Chatto & Windus.

We are four very different cooks. Claudia Roden, an acknowledged expert on Middle Eastern and Mediterranean food, brings an exotic flavour to the pages, while Weekend Cook Thane Prince, drawing on her years of experience in catering and as a working mother, writes inventively about family cooking. Simone Sekers, as her many cookery books testify, is an excellent cook in her own right; her recipes, a few of which I have also included, are firmly based in the best tradition of genuine home cooking. My own particular passion is the kitchen garden and cooking fresh, seasonal produce in light, healthy but flavourful ways. I also have a particular affection for what I can only describe as comfort food, the kind which satisfies the soul and is full of savour.

Given such a mix, it became clear from the beginning that this was to be no ordinary anthology of recipes. As themes leapt out of the pages, I realised that here was a unique opportunity to gather together a collection of recipes unrivalled in their variety and diversity. Here, at last, I thought, was a book which not only reflected modern ideas and interests but which genuinely offered something for everyone, from the health-conscious modern mum to the widely travelled gourmet, as well as those of us who enjoy cooking plain food well and hanker after honest dishes which have stood the test of time. Whether it was a simple supper dish, something exotic from the Lebanon, how to roast a goose, a quick and tasty way of cooking lamb chops, or an explanation of how to buy polenta or make rowan jelly, it could all be collected in one volume.

The book excited me for another reason. Though the title takes its name from the fact that our cookery pieces appeared in the Weekend section of the paper, it could not be more fortuitous because cooking at the weekend is its central theme. In modern busy lives, the weekend is the one time when families are together, when meals can be shared and enjoyed in a relaxed manner. It's also the occasion for entertaining and catching up with friends, when cooking can be regarded as a pleasure

2

rather than a necessity. But modern weekends are also full of activity, out-door pursuits and hobbies to be followed, children's parties to be fitted in, unexpected visitors to be catered for and picnics to be packed and unpacked a hundred times. Amid all this, the modern cook does not necessarily want to spend long hours either in the kitchen or searching for the right ingredients.

In short, cooks today want to provide interesting fresh food which tastes good but which readily fits into their family's lifestyle. To paraphrase that well-known saying, the modern cook (and rightly so, in my opinion) wants to bake his or her cake and have the time to be able to enjoy it. This is what *The Weekend Cookbook* is about. If there is a thread throughout the way each of us cooks, it is the belief that good fresh food, cooked simply and sympathetically, cannot be bettered. These are the kind of recipes you will find here, whether they are new or old favourites, familiar or exotic. None is beyond the competence of any average cook, many can be cooked in advance, and most take very little preparation.

The chapters are arranged around seven themes, each containing a wide variety of recipes hot and cold, from starters to desserts, and including meat and fish dishes as well as those suitable for vegetarians (marked throughout with a ⓥ). The recipes in each section are by no means mutually exclusive. Many in the chapter on Weekend Cooking, for example, would also fit admirably into Al Fresco Eating, and vice versa, as is indeed the case throughout the book, so that you may well find just what you're looking for in the section on Christmas, or Impromptu Food.

The index has been designed so that you can look up both the individual dish and the ingredient under various headings, such as soups or sauces, etc. Occasionally, if it seems particularly relevant to do so, I have indicated where other suitable recipes may be found.

Enjoy the book, for it is meant to be used, and I hope that it will find a permanent place in your kitchen. This is what I have striven for and what all the contributors wish for more than anything else. *Bon appétit*, and happy cooking!

WEIGHTS AND MEASUREMENTS

In common with many cooks, I have spent my life measuring ingredients using the traditional British Imperial system, this being the system with which I am familiar and comfortable. Surprisingly, this is also the method most of the people I talk with use, even those who may be ten or fifteen years younger than me and have been taught metric measurements at school. As both are included here as a matter of course, using British

Imperial or metric presents no difficulties, as long as you remember to use only one system throughout a recipe. In converting one to the other, I have taken one ounce to be 28.35 grammes (the actual conversion figure), rounding up to the nearest whole number, figuring that those who feel happier with the metric system can, for practical purposes, make any slight measuring adjustments in the kitchen as they · wish. Spoon measurements are level unless otherwise indicated; similarly, unless the recipe states otherwise, fresh herbs are used throughout the book.

I have always felt that, in writing a recipe, it is of paramount importance to pay particular attention to the details which really count. To this end I have tried to set out the recipes as clearly as I can. But I also know, only too well, that cooking is as much an art as a science, and that except for cakes and very small quantities, for most purposes strict adherence to quantities (or the size of your egg) is not as important as judgement and feel. No one expresses this better than Claudia Roden does in her book *Mediterranean Food*, in which she advises:

> Use measures, temperatures and timing as a guide but do not abandon your judgement, initiative and good sense and, above all, your taste. It is impossible to give foolproof measurements and instructions which cover every eventuality. You may have several things in your oven at the same time so that some of the shelves may not receive very much heat. A very large lemon could have little juice, or it may have plenty but not be sharp at all. Your garlic may be young or old, your aubergine bitter or not. Nature is like that. What is sharp or spicy or delicate for me may not be so for you; we all have different ideas about what is crisp or golden or brown so it is unlikely that your dish will turn out exactly like mine or even that it will come out exactly the same each time. But it is precisely that personal touch, that knack of doing things which is what cooking is all about. You will have to learn to trust your taste and to be confident about your judgement even if you have never eaten the dish before. . . . Like tuning a musical instrument, you must play it by ear.

That, I should like to feel, is the guiding spirit of this book also.

LYNDA BROWN

A NOTE ON CLING FILM

As a precautionary measure, it is recommended that cling film should not come in contact with foods. It should specifically not be used to wrap fatty foods such as cheese. Extra-safe formula cling film or low migration cling film should be used in the kitchen. Where cling film has been used in the book, substitutes have also been given.

Weekend Cooking

HOME-MADE BREAD

Nothing beats home-made bread. Anyone who makes it regularly – including Simone Sekers, Thane Prince and myself – will tell you nothing could be simpler. It freezes well and can be fitted into whatever schedule is convenient (bread essentially makes itself) for the dough can be left for hours if necessary and will come to no harm. Now that it has been given the dietary seal of approval, bread is very much a nineties' food. It makes sense to make your own at weekends, when the family can really appreciate it and everyone can discover how satisfying good bread can be. To get you started, here are some introductory remarks about bread flour and yeast from Simone Sekers.

Bread flours: Use wholemeal flour for flavour and fibre, and white for a lighter texture. Wholemeal and wholewheat flours are substantially the same thing and are usually labelled '100 per cent extraction', a misleading phrase which actually indicates the opposite – that the flour contains the wholewheat grain and that nothing has been extracted. Ordinary brown flour usually has an extraction rate of 85 per cent; granary flour is brown flour with malted wheat grains added for extra flavour. White flour labelled 'strong' is the one to use for breadmaking. It has more protein than the 'soft' white flours used for cakes and biscuits. Stoneground flour is ground between millstones and has more flavour and a coarser texture than flour made by the roller mill process, thus producing bread with much more character.

Yeast: Fresh yeast makes by far the best bread, but it is not always easily available. Supermarkets have been slow to supply it, although they are now good at supplying bread flours and dried yeast. Some that have in-store bakeries might sell you some, otherwise it can be bought from wholefood shops. (Bakers are sometimes reluctant to sell it and often charge too much.) It keeps well in the freezer, very well wrapped in the quantities you are likely to use it – say, 15, 30 or 45g/½, 1 or 1½oz portions. To use, simply defrost it in a little warm water, then make this up to the total liquid needed for the recipe. Dried yeast is much more readily available, and comes in two sorts – that which is mixed straight into the flour and needs only one rising, and that which needs to be dissolved in warm water first. You need twice as much fresh yeast as dried.

SIMONE SEKERS

Editor's note: When buying wholemeal flour, buy the kind milled from organically grown wheat if possible. This is free of any pesticide residues that may have been sprayed on the crops in the field, or on the grain during storage.

Household triple bread

Makes 2 large or 4 small loaves

450g/1lb each of stoneground wholemeal, strong plain,
and granary bread flour
3 tsp fine sea salt
45g/1½oz fresh yeast
approx. 900ml/1½pt warm water
3 tbsp sunflower oil

This is my own recipe for the bread we eat every day. Mix the flours with the salt in a roomy bowl. Mix the yeast into a little of the water until it has dissolved, and then add the rest of the water. Make a well in the middle of the flour and pour in almost all the water and yeast mixture. Mix well together into a dough, adding more water if the dough seems too stiff to work comfortably, or more flour if it is too wet and sticks to your fingers. Knead thoroughly, for as long as you can, but not less than 5 minutes. Form the dough into a ball, cut a cross right through it and leave to prove in the mixing bowl. Wrap the whole bowl in a large polythene bag and put it somewhere warm such as the airing cupboard to rise.

When the dough has doubled in size (this will take about 1½–2 hours depending on the warmth of the surrounding atmosphere), take it out and knead again. Divide into two or four, depending on the size of your bread tins, and form each piece into a long sausage shape. Double the ends underneath and fit the dough into the tins. Leave to prove in the same manner as before, until the dough reaches the top of the tin. Bake in a preheated, very hot oven (230°C/450°F/gas mark 8) for 30–45 minutes. Fan-operated ovens take less time – allow 30 minutes for a 900g/2lb loaf. When it is cooked, the bread will sound hollow when tapped.

For bread with a soft crust, wrap the loaf in a teacloth as it cools. Soft-crusted bread is also best for freezing, as a crisp crust may break away from the bread when the loaf is thawed. In cold weather warm the mixing bowl and flours in a low oven before you start.

SIMONE SEKERS

Editor's note: Dough likes a snug warm atmosphere best, but will rise perfectly well in cooler conditions, although it will take longer. This can be an advantage if you don't want to make the bread until later in the day. Never, however, leave the dough by a hot fire or propped on top of a radiator – too much heat will kill the yeast and make the dough sticky. Keeping back a small lump of dough every time, say 110g/4oz, to add to your next batch of dough progressively improves the character of the bread and the rising ability of subsequent doughs. Wrap it in a plastic bag and freeze until required. Either let it thaw naturally, or pop it into some of the warm liquid. Add to the flour with the water and incorporate in the usual way.

Mary Lou's Magimix bread

This recipe was passed on to me by a friend, and requires no mixing or kneading. Any standard bread recipe works well. Using molasses instead of sugar gives a rich flavour and colour to the bread.

Makes 1 large loaf

450g/1lb wholemeal or a mixture of bread flours
1 generous tsp active dried yeast
1/2 tsp salt
1 tsp sugar (optional)
1 tbsp oil (optional)
approx. 300ml/10fl. oz warm water

Put the dough attachment into the food processor. Put the flour, yeast, salt, and sugar if using, into the bowl and process for a few seconds to distribute the dry ingredients. Add the oil if using. Add the water through the funnel while the motor is running and process for 1–2 minutes until the mixture forms a soft dough. Leave to double in size in the bowl, about 1½–2 hours (it can be left longer if more convenient), covering up the funnel with the funnel attachment to create a sealed atmosphere. Turn out, knead lightly, shape as described in the recipe for Household triple bread above, and put into a warmed oiled 900g/2lb loaf tin. Oil the top, leave in a warm place until the dough has come to the top of the tin and bake as described on p. 10.

LYNDA BROWN

Brioche

Traditional recipes for brioche can be daunting. This is an easy version from Thane Prince for weekend breakfasts and brunches.

Makes 10 small brioche

225g/8oz plain flour
1 pkt easy blend yeast
3 tbsp milk
100g/3¹/₂oz melted butter
1 tsp sugar
¹/₂ tsp salt
2 beaten eggs (plus 1 egg to glaze)

Put all the ingredients into a bowl and mix until it forms a soft dough; in a food processor this will take 2–3 minutes. Turn out the dough and knead lightly (it will be sticky). Put into a greased polythene bag and leave to rise either for 2 hours in a warm place or overnight in the refrigerator. Knock back the dough, reserving one sixth, and divide the remainder into 10 balls.

Knead each one lightly and place in buttered brioche pans. If not available, you could use deep bun tins. Top each with a small ball of dough from the reserved batch and glaze with beaten egg. Cover and allow to rise again until nearly doubled in size. Bake in a preheated hot oven, 220°C/425°F/gas mark 7, for 10–15 minutes until well browned.

THANE PRINCE

Scottish oatcakes

These crisp oatcakes from Thane Prince have become a favourite in my household, and they could easily be made by children.

Serves 4

110g/4oz fine oatmeal
pinch of salt
15g/¹/₂oz lard
approx. 60ml/2fl. oz boiling water

Put the oats, salt and fat into a food processor and mix for 60 seconds. Add the boiling water and continue to process for a further 90 seconds.

Turn out the paste on to a lightly floured board and knead lightly. While the dough is still warm, roll out to a thickness of 3mm/⅛ in and cut into rounds or triangles. Transfer to a baking sheet and bake in a preheated oven, 160°C/325°F/gas mark 3, for 15 minutes until crisp but only lightly coloured. Alternatively, cook the oatcakes on top of the stove on a griddle or in a non-stick pan over a medium heat for about 5 minutes. If cooked this way, they should not be turned. Serve warm with preserves or cheese. Any remaining can be stored in an airtight container. Warm through first before using.

Note: Regular porridge oats can be substituted if you use the metal blade of a food processor.

THANE PRINCE

BRUNCH

Brunch, as Thane Prince commented in an article devoted to the subject, is a transatlantic idea that well suits the increasingly popular preference here for active weekends. My own feeling is that as weekday breakfasts become perfunctory affairs, breakfast at the weekend is already nudging amiably towards brunch, which has the spirit of an old-fashioned British breakfast trimmed to suit modern tastes and appetites. The emphasis, Thane adds, should be on the light and tempting. Compôtes, kedgerees, home-made breads and soufflés immediately come to mind; so do fish cakes, creamy home-made yoghurt, plenty of fresh fruit, milky soft fresh cheeses, and warm crisp oatcakes spread with preserves.

Breakfast (or brunch) dried-fruit compôte

This compôte improves beautifully with age and will keep for a week in the refrigerator. The proportion of fruits can be altered to suit. Serve on its own or with a few segments of fresh orange, peel and pith carefully removed.

Serves 8

225g/8oz large prunes, pitted or whole
225g/8oz other dried fruits (choose some of the following: apricots, pears, figs, peaches, apple rings)
plus, optionally, up to 55g/2oz of some of the following:
dried pineapple, papaya, large raisins, 1–2 tsp chopped
crystallised ginger
1.2l/2pt weak, good-quality Indian tea such as Assam
2.5cm/1in stick of cinnamon
6–8 allspice berries, or 2–3 cloves
large strip of scrubbed orange or tangerine rind
30–55g/1–2oz soft brown sugar (optional)

Rinse the dried fruit in hot water and put into a large bowl. Strain the tea into a pan, add the chosen seasonings and simmer for 5 minutes to allow the flavours to infuse. Pour over the fruit, cover and leave for a minimum of 24, and preferably 36, hours before eating. During this time the fruit softens and forms its own delicious syrup as some of the sugars and flavours seep into the liquid. No extra sugar should be necessary but, if you prefer, 30–55g/1–2oz soft brown sugar can be added when you soak the fruit.

LYNDA BROWN

Rhubarb with honey and rose-water

Serves 4

450g/1lb young rhubarb
120ml/4fl. oz water
2–4 tbsp honey, or to taste
1–2 tbsp rose-water

Choose a pan which will take the rhubarb in a single layer. Gradually bring the rhubarb, water and honey to the boil, and simmer very gently until just cooked. Allow to cool, then stir in rose-water to taste. Serve with yoghurt.

THANE PRINCE

Editor's note: Pink forced rhubarb, available from December to March, is especially good for compôtes. It tastes more delicate and tender than ordinary rhubarb, needs less sweetening and keeps its dazzling pink colour when cooked. It will need hardly any poaching: bring gently to the boil, cover, turn off the heat and allow to cool. By the time it has cooled it will be ready.

Home-made yoghurt

Home-made yoghurt is far superior to bought yoghurt, marvellous for breakfast with honey or fruit, much cheaper and idiotically easy to make. Any kind of milk can be used, though full-cream milk produces the best flavour; for an extra rich yoghurt, you may like to follow Thane Prince's suggestion and use a mixture of cream and milk. A yoghurt maker is most convenient, and to be recommended if you make yoghurt regularly, but is not necessary. A vacuum flask set aside for yoghurt (the yoghurt tends to stick to the sides which is not good for the tea or coffee), or a well-insulated bowl kept in a warm place, works perfectly well. On holidays I have often made yoghurt in a bowl covered with cling film and left in a gently warmed through, turned-off oven, which works a treat.

Two things only are needed for success. To make your first batch you need a little plain live yoghurt to act as the starter – scrutinise bought yoghurts carefully (pasteurised yoghurt will not work) – and somewhere with a constant temperature of around 45–50°C/110–120°F. Depending on the strength of the starter and the incubating temperature it will take anything between 3 and 8 hours to set. Generally, the longer the yoghurt

15

is left to incubate, the sharper the flavour and the more the whey will separate out; experiment to find which you like best. The first couple of times, make it using 600ml/1pt milk. Thereafter, once you've got the feel of it, 1.2l/2pt of milk is a more convenient quantity.

Bring 600ml/1pt of milk to the boil. Cool until it feels just comfortably warm to your finger, or very slightly hotter (higher temperatures will kill the bacteria). Mix 1 tbsp plain live yoghurt with a little of the cooled milk, then mix this into the rest of the milk, stirring well. If you are using separate yoghurt pots and a yoghurt maker, simply stir 1 tsp of yoghurt into each pot of cooled milk. If you do not have a yoghurt maker, pour the mixture into a vacuum flask and screw on the lid, or transfer to a warm covered bowl and put somewhere well insulated. Once the yoghurt has set to your liking, transfer to the refrigerator. It will keep for up to a week. For continuing good results, make the next batch while the present yoghurt is fresh, preferably within three days, stirring well before taking out a tablespoon as a starter.

Home-made yoghurt is thinner than bought yoghurt. If you prefer a thicker yoghurt, either stir in up to 55g/2oz skimmed-milk powder per 600ml/1pt of milk, or simmer the milk first until reduced in volume by at least a quarter and preferably a half. This produces a yoghurt similar to the rich Greek-style yoghurt.

Another way to enjoy home-made yoghurt is to strain it through a sieve lined with muslin set over a bowl to catch the drips until it is the thickness of soft cheese. This is *laban*, or *labna*, the yoghurt cheese much appreciated throughout the Middle East. Season very lightly with salt, roll it into little balls and keep under olive oil. Served plain, or scattered with a little mint, fresh or dried, and a little of its oil, these are excellent for brunch or for a light lunch with good bread and ripe tomatoes taken on the patio on a nice sunny day.

LYNDA BROWN

French toast with fresh fruit

Serves 4

8 slices day-old French bread (or other white bread)
2 eggs, beaten with 150ml/5fl. oz creamy milk
450g/1lb fresh fruit: strawberries, peaches, nectarines, etc.
caster sugar to taste
1–2 tbsp butter and a little oil for frying

Put the slices of bread to soak in the egg and milk mixture in a shallow dish for at least 10 minutes. Meanwhile, slice the fruit, remove stones as necessary and sprinkle with sugar. Heat the butter and oil in a large frying pan and shallow fry the bread slices, a few at a time, until golden on both sides. Serve with the prepared fruit.   THANE PRINCE

Glyn Christian's kedgeree with quails' eggs

Serves 6–8

900g/2lb naturally smoked Finnan haddock
1 bay leaf
110g/4oz butter
225g/8oz long grain rice
1 tsp ground coriander
½ tsp ground cumin
½ tsp turmeric
12 hard-boiled quails' eggs

Put the fish in a pan with the bay leaf, cover well with cold water and bring slowly to the boil. Remove from the heat and check that the fish is cooked by easing it from the bone (if not quite cooked, leave in the hot water a little longer). Take the fish from the pan, reserving the cooking liquor, and flake, taking care to remove all skin and bone. Melt 1 tbsp butter in a saucepan, stir in the rice and cook for 2–3 minutes until it looks translucent. Add 600ml/1pt of the fish poaching liquid, cover and cook until all the liquid is absorbed and the rice is soft, about 20 minutes.

Once the rice has cooked, melt the remaining butter and sweat the spices in it for a couple of minutes. Stir into the warm rice, mixing lightly and evenly, followed by the fish and then the eggs. Do this very gently to avoid breaking everything up. Serve hot.   THANE PRINCE

Editor's note: This is a fragrant, buttery, luxurious kedgeree. If you cannot find quails' eggs (or find them too fiddly), 4 coarsely chopped hard-boiled free-range eggs are just as good. If you prefer, the amount of butter may be halved without any loss of flavour.

Simone Sekers writes: QUAILS' EGGS are much cheaper and easier to find than they were, as quail are now farmed on a large scale. They are often stocked by butchers and fishmongers, as well as good grocers and delicatessens. Although they add glamour to a meal, allow plenty of time for peeling them as they are fiddly, and especially so while still warm. Alternatively, you can serve them in their attractive speckled shells and let your guests do the work.

See also: Smoked haddock and cumin soufflé, p. 70.

INFORMAL ENTERTAINING

Entertaining at home is one of the most pleasurable aspects of cooking at the weekend. Modern dinner parties feature lighter, inventive, less elaborate though still stylish food, and are relaxed informal affairs where the food, wine and company are equal partners. In this section I have tried to bring together a few dishes which would suit such occasions, and which are special enough to grace any table. You will find others in the chapters on game and fish as well as the chapters on outdoor food and the French and Italian Connection.

Melon, apple and tarragon cream soup (√)

This is a refreshing instant soup, perfect as a light starter for a summer meal.

Serves 4

225g/8oz ripe fragrant melon, cut into chunks
300ml/10fl. oz apple juice
60–90ml/2–3fl. oz double cream, or to taste
1–2 tsp finely chopped tarragon, or to taste

Blend the melon chunks and apple juice to a smooth cream. Stir in double cream and finely chopped tarragon to taste. Add extra melon, cut into small cubes. Serve chilled, in pretty soup cups or small dishes.

LYNDA BROWN

Simone Sekers writes: APPLE JUICE: For this recipe you must choose your apple juice carefully – many varieties are over-sweet and sometimes made from apple concentrate. Look for a brand such as Peake's Organic apple juice from Suffolk (widely distributed and available from good supermarkets and wholefood shops). If in doubt, buy unsweetened apple juice in a carton from the cold cabinet of the supermarket, rather than that in a box labelled 'long life'.

Patricia Hegarty's fennel and Jerusalem artichoke soup

This is a slightly simplified version of one of the many excellent soups they serve at Hope End Hotel near Ledbury, famous for its remarkable kitchen garden. A good winter dinner-party soup.

1 bulb of Florence fennel, sliced
15g/½oz butter
1 medium onion, chopped
225g/8oz Jerusalem artichokes, peeled and sliced
850ml/1½pt ham or chicken stock, or water if no stock
is available
1 tsp fennel seeds, crushed and pounded
up to 150ml/5fl. oz single cream
seasoning

Reserve some of the feathery fennel fronds for garnish. Melt the butter and cook the onion until soft, and then add the fennel, artichokes and stock or water. Cover and simmer until soft, about 15–20 minutes. Add the crushed fennel seeds, then blend the soup in a blender or food processor until smooth. Reheat, adjusting the consistency if necessary and adding cream and seasoning to taste. Serve with a scattering of chopped fennel fronds on top.

Note: Stock produces a richer soup, water a thinner but cleaner-tasting soup.

LYNDA BROWN

Avocado with apple, prawns and horseradish dressing

Serves 4

For the filling
55g/2oz best prawns, defrosted and chopped into
sizeable pieces
1/2 red eating apple, cored and cut into tiny dice
juice of 1/2 lemon

For the dressing
1 tbsp mayonnaise
1 dsp thick Greek yoghurt, sheep's milk for preference
1 dsp freshly grated horseradish, plus
extra lemon juice to taste

2 ripe avocados
tiny sprigs of watercress or twists of lemon for
decoration

Mix the prawns with the apple and toss both in lemon juice. Make the dressing by mixing all the ingredients, sharpening with lemon juice to taste. Cut each avocado in half, lightly fill with the prawn and apple mixture, spoon over the dressing, decorate and serve immediately.

LYNDA BROWN

Simone Sekers writes: HORSERADISH, freshly grated, has a pungency that most commercially prepared sauces do not have, so it is worth making the most of it when you can get a whole root. Grate it, then open freeze it before wrapping it well. It can then be used to flavour whipped cream, crème fraîche or Greek yoghurt, to partner beef or smoked trout.

Creamy basil custards ⓥ

Serves 4

30g/1oz basil leaves, stripped from their stalks
2 large eggs
180ml/6fl. oz creamy milk
4 level tbsp thick plain yoghurt, preferably the Greek
sheep's-milk variety
butter for greasing

For the sauce
225g/8oz very ripe tomatoes, skinned
7g/¼oz butter
1 clove garlic, crushed

Reserve 4 of the basil leaves for decoration and chop the rest in a food processor. (Alternatively, chop by hand, then pound to a paste with a pestle and mortar.) Add the eggs, milk and yoghurt and process for 2–3 minutes until absolutely smooth and the basil is reduced to speckles. Divide between 4 well-buttered small ramekin dishes. Put in a pan with water to come nearly up to the rims and bake at 160°C/325°F/gas mark 3 for 40 minutes, or until the centres feel just firm to the touch.

Meanwhile, chop the tomatoes and cook gently in the butter with the garlic for 5–7 minutes. Remove the garlic and blend the tomatoes to form a light sauce. Run a palette knife round the edge of the ramekin dishes, then invert on to 4 hot plates, giving a gentle shake downwards. Spoon around the sauce and decorate with a basil leaf. Serve as a first course.

Note: Timing can be tricky for these delectable fragile custards, which should be just set and very creamy; be prepared to experiment at first to get the desired consistency.

LYNDA BROWN

Monsieur Commandré's duck breasts with honey and cider vinegar

This French recipe, and the dish that follows, are both quick, easy dishes, ideal for dinners *à deux*.

Serves 2 (or 4 as a first course)

2 large duck breasts (Gressingham duck is ideal)
1 tbsp honey
1 tbsp cider vinegar
4–6 tbsp concentrated duck or meat stock
approx. 30g/1oz diced unsalted butter
young salad leaves, plus a few walnut halves

Heat a non-stick frying pan and seal the duck breasts, skin side down, for 2–3 minutes. Turn and seal the other side likewise. Reduce the heat, mop up any excess fat with kitchen paper, cover and cook for 2–3 minutes longer.

Turn off the heat and let the meat relax for 4–5 minutes. Remove and keep warm while you make the sauce: stir the honey into the meat juices, followed by the vinegar and stock. Reduce slightly, then swirl in butter to taste to give a glossy sauce. Cut the duck breasts into thin diagonal slices, arrange on hot plates and pour over the glaze. Decorate with salad leaves and walnuts. Serves four as a first course, or two as a main dish accompanied with rice.

LYNDA BROWN

Simone Sekers writes: GRESSINGHAM DUCK is a fine gastronomic development from Lancashire, combining the flavour of wild duck with the more succulent meat of the domestic bird, but with less fat. There is just enough fat to produce a good crisp skin. It is widely available now, from good butchers.

Noisettes of lamb with mint and ruby glaze

Serves 4

4 noisettes of lamb, taken from the loin, approximately
2.5cm/1in thick
7g/¹⁄₄oz clarified butter plus 1 dsp vegetable oil for
frying

For the glaze
240ml/8fl. oz red wine
1 sprig mint
1¹⁄₂ tbsp redcurrant jelly, or to taste
30g/1oz butter, cut into bits
1 tsp finely chopped mint, plus extra for garnish

Cook the lamb in the butter and oil over a brisk heat in a non-stick frying pan for approximately 2 minutes each side. Remove and keep warm on 4 hot plates. Wipe out any fat. Pour in the wine, add the sprig of mint and reduce by half. Turn down the heat to low and stir in redcurrant jelly to taste. Remove the mint and, off the heat, bind the sauce with the butter, shaking the pan to amalgamate the sauce. Stir in the chopped mint and pour a little of the dark shiny glaze around each noisette. Decorate with a mint leaf and serve immediately with rice. French beans or spinach make good accompaniments.

LYNDA BROWN

Roast loin of lamb savoyard

Herb crusts have become fashionable of late. This is a nutty variation. The herb crust can be made in advance, and the lamb prepared for roasting well ahead of time.

Serves 2–3

1 loin of lamb in a piece (not chined),
approx. 4–5 chops thick

For the herb crust
45g/1½oz soft breadcrumbs
30g/1oz ground walnuts
1 tbsp finely chopped thyme
30g/1oz melted butter
1 tbsp water/wine/vermouth

If not already removed, cut the breast flap from the loin (this can be cooked slowly with beans for a cheap mid-week supper), and remove all the fat. Roast on its side, loin uppermost, in a hot oven, 220°C/425°F/gas mark 7, for 20–25 minutes, depending on thickness. Do not overcook. Remove from the oven and let it rest for 10 minutes.

Meanwhile, thoroughly mix all the ingredients for the crust to form a paste. Spread over the back of the loin, patting it on firmly with your hands to form a smooth thin layer. Place under a hot grill, about 10cm/4in from the heat, and cook for 6–8 minutes or until the crust is evenly browned.

Serve on its side, carving into long thin slices at the table: the crust invariably comes away but tastes delicious. The tender nugget of under-fillet should be sliced across into even portions (or it can be removed and used for a mid-week stir-fry). Spinach and Farçon savoyard (*see* p. 185) make splendid accompaniments.

Note: To serve 4, buy a whole loin (6–7 chops) and increase the ingredients for the herb crust by half.

LYNDA BROWN

Poussins with couscous stuffing

These, writes Claudia Roden, are one of the great delicacies of Moroccan cuisine: 'Served at feasts and celebrations, they are presented on great platters around a mountain of extra stuffing. The sweet stuffing is characteristic of the cooking of Fez. You can leave the sugar out if you prefer, but I recommend you try it. To make it easier for yourself, if you do not want to stuff the birds, you can prepare and serve the stuffing separately.'

Serves 4

For the stuffing
450g/1lb couscous
salt
1–2 tbsp caster sugar
3 tbsp sunflower oil
1½ tbsp cinnamon
2 tbsp orange-flower water (*see* p. 210)
3 tbsp raisins, soaked in warm water for 10 minutes
110g/4oz blanched almonds

4 poussins
3 tbsp butter or sunflower oil
1–2 large onions, grated
2 cloves garlic, crushed
2 tsp cinnamon
¼ tsp ginger
½ tsp powdered saffron (*see* p. 69)
salt
300ml/10fl. oz water
2 tbsp honey

Start with the stuffing: moisten the couscous with a little less than its volume of lightly salted water – about 360–450ml/12–15fl. oz. Stir well so that it is evenly absorbed. After about 5 minutes, stir in the sugar, 2 tbsp oil, the cinnamon and orange-flower water, and the drained raisins. Fry the almonds in the remaining oil, chop them coarsely and add to the stuffing. Fill each poussin with about 3 tbsp of stuffing. They should not be too tightly packed or the stuffing may burst out. Sew up the skin at both ends using cotton thread (or use cocktail sticks) so that it overlaps the openings. Reserve the remaining stuffing.

To cook the poussins, melt the butter or oil in a wide heavy saucepan, and add the onions, garlic, cinnamon, ginger, saffron and salt. Arrange the poussins on top and add the water. Simmer gently, covered, for about

30 minutes or until the birds are tender, adding more water if necessary. Turn them over at least once, finishing breast side down so that they are well impregnated with the sauce and its flavours. Lift one out (to make a little room) and stir in the honey, then return it to the pan and continue to cook them until the flesh is at 'melting tenderness' and can be easily pulled off the bone, around another 15–30 minutes.

Heat the reserved stuffing in a saucepan, adding a little extra water if necessary to prevent sticking until the couscous is plump and tender. Alternatively, heat in a covered dish in the oven. To serve, make a mountain of the stuffing on a platter and place the birds and their sauce around it.

CLAUDIA RODEN

Simone Sekers writes: COUSCOUS is semolina which has been specially treated: a flattening and damping process enlarges the grains, which are then dusted with wheat flour. This process ensures that the grains remain separate when moistened and steamed as part of the traditional North African couscous. Almost all available here is precooked, and needs only the addition of water and heating through carefully. It is available fairly widely, in wholefood shops and delicatessens if not supermarkets.

VALENTINE'S DAY FEAST

This menu, with its decidedly romantic theme, was put together by Thane Prince to celebrate St Valentine's day. It is such a lovely menu I have left it in its entirety – though each of the dishes would happily partner many others in the book also.

All the preparation can be done in advance or the day before, leaving only the pastry hearts and vegetables to be cooked on the evening.

Marinated salmon with mint

Serves 2

110g/4oz very fresh raw salmon, boned and skinned
juice of 1 lemon
juice of 1 blood orange
pinch of caster sugar
salt and pepper to taste
1 tbsp finely sliced fresh mint

Slice the salmon with a very sharp knife as thinly as possible. Arrange in a serving dish and pour over the juices mixed with the sugar and a little salt. Grind over some black pepper and sprinkle over the mint. Leave to marinate overnight. Serve with crisp brown bread rolls.

Tudor spiced chicken in puff pastry hearts

The idea for this dish comes from *Elinor Fettiplace's Cookbook*, by Hilary Spurling.

Serves 2

170g/6oz skinned, boned chicken breast
45g/1½oz raisins
a few blades of mace
2.5cm/1in stick of cinnamon
approx. 210ml/7fl. oz each white wine and water
pinch of saffron (*see* p. 69)

For the sauce
1 tbsp butter
2 shallots
30g/1oz pine nuts
1 clove garlic, chopped
1 tbsp flour
4 tbsp double cream
salt and pepper to taste

To finish
225g/8oz ready-made puff pastry
beaten egg to glaze

Place the chicken, raisins, mace and cinnamon in a saucepan and just cover with wine and water. Bring to the simmer and cook for about 10 minutes. Leave everything in the pan to cool and once cold remove the chicken and raisins to a plate. Discard the whole spices, reduce the liquid to a scant 150ml/5fl. oz, and mix in the saffron. Cut the chicken into 1.25cm/½in dice.

For the sauce, melt the butter in a pan and fry the shallots, stirring until they start to turn light golden brown. Add the pine nuts and garlic and continue frying and stirring until the nuts just begin to colour. Stir in the flour and when well combined with the butter add the cream and reduced stock. Cook, still stirring, until you have a thick sauce, about 4–5 minutes. Season well with salt and pepper and then lightly stir in the chicken and raisins. Leave this filling until cold.

Roll the pastry into an oblong. Make a paper template or cut free-hand 4 12.5cm/5in hearts from the dough (save the remaining pastry for cheese straws. Divide the filling and spoon on to two hearts and brush the edges with water. Roll the two remaining hearts to make them a little larger, and place them over the filling, pressing the edges together well to seal. Make two tiny cuts in the top to allow the steam to escape while cooking. Place on a baking sheet and cover with cling film or foil until needed.

Forty minutes before eating, preheat the oven to 220°C/425°F/gas mark 7. Brush the hearts with beaten egg and cook for 30 minutes until golden brown. Serve with a green vegetable.

Passion fruit sorbet in ginger baskets

Serves 4

85g/3oz sugar
240ml/8fl. oz water
4 passion fruit
juice of 1 lemon

For the ginger-snap biscuits (makes 10 baskets)
55g/2oz each of demerara sugar, butter, golden syrup,
and plain flour
1 tsp ground ginger
2 oranges

For the sorbet, dissolve the sugar and water in a medium saucepan and bring to the boil. Cook for 4 minutes to form a syrup. Remove from the heat and allow to cool. Cut the passion fruit in half and scrape the seeds out into a sieve set over a bowl. With a spoon press as much juice through the sieve as you can. Stir the syrup and lemon juice into the passion fruit juice, pour into a freezer container and freeze for 4–6 hours, stirring well with a fork every hour to break up the ice crystals (or see p. 29). When the sorbet is frozen, cover until needed.

For the ginger-snap biscuits, preheat the oven to 160°C/325°F/gas mark 3. Melt the sugar, butter and syrup in a saucepan and remove from the heat. Stir in the flour and ginger, mixing well. Grease a large baking sheet and on it drop 2 dsp of mixture, placing them well apart. Bake for 7–8 minutes until golden brown.

Have the oranges ready on a board. Remove the tray from the oven and allow the ginger snaps to cool for 1–2 minutes. Slip a palette knife under one biscuit and quickly but carefully lay it on top of an orange, moulding it slightly to fit. Flatten the bottom of the 'basket' and repeat with the other biscuit. Don't worry if you can't manage the first time: there is sufficient mixture to make several biscuits, so keep trying.

As soon as the 'baskets' are cool, and while the next batch is cooking, remove them carefully from the oranges. They can be stored in an airtight tin, right side up, for up to 3 days.

About 15 minutes before serving, move the sorbet to the fridge to soften a little. Place a basket on each plate and spoon in the sorbet. If desired, decorate with fresh fruit or flowers.

THANE PRINCE

FAMILY SUPPERS

Sausages and mash with some crisp cabbage make a very good family supper, as do all our well-known favourites. But there are many other dishes that also fit the bill which are fun to do from time to time. The following group of recipes has been chosen with this in mind.

Though they take their inspiration from near and far, the recipes use essentially familiar foods to make familiar dishes – an important requirement for family food which has to try to suit everyone – but with a different twist here and there, as with the up-to-the-minute creamy vegetarian quiche and adaptable stuffed peppers, both from Thane Prince.

Broccoli and sun-dried tomato quiche (√)

Serves 6

225g/8oz shortcrust pastry
225g/8oz broccoli florets
6–8 sun-dried tomatoes, chopped (*see* note, below)
3 eggs
300ml/10fl. oz single cream
black pepper

Line a 23cm/9in flan dish with the pastry. Blanch the broccoli in boiling water for 60 seconds, drain and refresh in cold water. Drain well.

Scatter the tomato pieces over the pastry case and top with the broccoli. Beat the eggs with the cream and season with black pepper – you will not need extra salt as the tomatoes are quite salty. Pour this over the vegetables and bake in the centre of a preheated oven, 190°C/375°F/gas mark 5, for 35–40 minutes until golden brown. Serve warm or cool with a fresh green salad.

THANE PRINCE

Simone Sekers writes: SUN-DRIED TOMATOES are the latest fashionable flavouring. They can be bought *au naturel* or preserved in oil. The former should be soaked before adding them to pasta sauces, or as pizza toppings, but can be simply chopped and added to any slow-cooking casserole. They add a very concentrated sweet tomato flavour, not unlike the effect of adding raisins or prunes to a dish. Those in oil can be added to salads, particularly any containing cheeses such as feta, mozzarella or mild goat's cheese. Good Italian delicatessens should stock them. Both varieties can be bought by post from Culpeper Ltd, Hadstock Rd, Linton, Cambridge CB1 6NJ, or at any one of their 17 shops.

Hungarian stuffed peppers

This dish doubles up conveniently as both a meat dish and, if there is a vegetarian in the family, as a vegetarian dish using cheese instead of pork. The peppers may be made in advance and reheated.

Serves 6

6 medium peppers, red or green, washed

For the stuffing
1 medium onion, chopped
30g/1oz lard
1 fat clove garlic
225g/8oz minced pork
225g/8oz rice cooked in 1.2l/2pt water and drained
1 beaten egg
salt and pepper

For the sauce
30g/1oz butter
30g/1oz flour
1 tsp salt
1 tsp sugar
450g/1lb tinned tomatoes, liquidised

Cut the tops off the peppers and reserve. Remove the seeds from the peppers and arrange them in a deep saucepan, standing upright. To make the stuffing, slowly fry the onion in the melted lard until golden; this will take about 15 minutes. Add the garlic and continue to fry for 1–2 minutes. Remove from the heat and mix in the pork, rice, beaten egg and seasoning. Stuff the peppers with the pork/rice mixture and put on the tops.

To make the sauce, melt the butter in a saucepan and add the flour. Stirring constantly, slowly brown the roux. When golden, add the tomatoes, then bring to the boil, mixing well. Pour around the peppers – there should be enough to come to the tops of the peppers; if not, add extra water. Simmer the peppers over a low heat for 1½ hours. Serve hot with bread or extra rice.

Vegetarian alternative: Omit the pork and substitute vegetable oil or butter for the lard. For each stuffed pepper, allow 55g/2oz cubed Emmental or Gruyère cheese and 1–2 tbsp pine nuts. Follow the recipe as described, browning the nuts lightly first and mixing the cheese and nuts into the rice.

THANE PRINCE

Latkes Ⓥ

Potato cakes come in various forms. These, from Russia, can be eaten on their own or with left-over meat (or sausages or bacon) and are good for high tea, snacks or brunch.

Serves 4–6

400g/14oz potatoes (peeled weight)
225g/8oz onion (peeled weight)
1 egg, beaten
3 tbsp plain flour
salt and freshly ground black pepper

Grate the potato and onion together, using either a food processor or hand grater. Pour off any liquid that forms in the bowl. Add the egg, flour and plenty of salt and pepper. Beat the mixture until everything is well combined. Heat about 1.25cm/½in oil in a frying pan and shallow-fry spoonfuls of the mixture, 2 or 3 at a time, for about 4 minutes, turning once. The edges will become crisp quite quickly, so turn the heat down if necessary to make sure the latkes are cooked through. Drain on absorbent paper and keep warm while you cook the remaining mixture. Serve with sour cream and apple sauce.

THANE PRINCE

Italian meatballs in tomato and sage sauce

Serves 4

450g/1lb lean braising steak, trimmed of fat, skin and
connective tissue (allow about 560g/1¼lb
before trimming)
55g/2oz freshly grated Parmesan cheese (*see* p. 197)
2 tbsp olive oil, plus extra 2 tbsp for frying
flour for dusting
2–3 sage leaves
340g/12oz tinned tomatoes
1 clove garlic, crushed

Cube the meat and process in a food processor, in batches, for a few seconds only so that it retains a slightly coarse texture. Alternatively, put through the coarse blade of the mincer. Transfer to a bowl, add the Parmesan and 2 tbsp olive oil and beat until well mixed. Form into 16 equal oval-shaped meatballs, dusting each one lightly with flour. Heat 2 tbsp olive oil with the sage in a non-stick frying pan and brown the meatballs all over on a moderate heat. Add the tomatoes and garlic, bring to the boil, cover, and cook gently for about 20–25 minutes. Remove the meatballs to a serving dish and boil down the sauce until thick. Pour around the meat and serve with pasta or rice, removing the garlic first if you wish.

LYNDA BROWN

Pot-roast chicken with potatoes, fennel and garlic

Serves 4

1.5kg/3lb chicken, preferably free range
1 large bulb fennel, coarsely chopped
1 onion, coarsely chopped
1 head garlic, cleaned but not peeled
1 bay leaf
1 tbsp olive oil
675–900g/1½–2lb small waxy potatoes, peeled and
parboiled for 3–4 minutes
90–120ml/3–4fl. oz dry vermouth
300ml/10fl. oz water
1 tsp potato flour (optional) (*ooo* p. 39)

Remove any fat from the cavity of the chicken and wash out the interior. In a large flame-proof dish, gently cook the fennel and onion with the garlic and bay leaf in the olive oil for about 5 minutes. Add the potatoes and pour in the vermouth and water (you could use the potato water). Sit the chicken on top, breast side down, cover very tightly and cook in a moderate oven, 180°C/350°F/gas mark 4, for 1¼–1½ hours, turning the chicken over halfway through.

Remove the chicken carefully, tipping the juices from the cavity back into the dish, and keep warm. Transfer the dish, still containing the sauce and vegetables, to the top of the stove and cook for a few minutes to concentrate the flavour, removing the fat by tipping the dish on its side and skimming off that which collects in the corner. Thicken slightly if you like, using potato flour slaked in a little cold water, and transfer to a serving dish. Carve the chicken, handing round the vegetables separately. The garlic can be removed before serving if you prefer.

LYNDA BROWN

Simone Sekers writes: FREE-RANGE CHICKENS are now an alternative to flavourless battery birds, and can be found in most supermarkets, as well as good butchers and poulterers. Free-range chickens appear under various brand names – for example, look for Landais chickens in Tesco and Duc de Bourgogne in Marks & Spencer. Maize-fed birds are also suitable for this recipe. The flesh of all these birds is firmer than that of battery hens, the flavour more pronounced and the price slightly higher.

The next three dishes from Claudia Roden are good examples of how foreign flavours can be incorporated into everyday eating. I especially recommend the Tunisian lamb and lemon stew, which sheds a whole new light on meat and potatoes. The first, a quick and easy Italian chicken dish, is a speciality of Naples.

Chicken with rosemary

Serves 4

1 chicken, weighing about 1.5kg/3lb, cut into quarters
45g/1½oz butter
1 tbsp sunflower or olive oil
2 large garlic cloves, cut in half
2 sprigs of rosemary
180ml/6fl. oz dry white wine
salt and pepper

Heat the butter and oil in a frying pan with the garlic and rosemary. When the mixture sizzles, put in the chicken and cook over a medium heat, turning the pieces to colour them all over. It is usual to remove the garlic and rosemary at this stage so that they lend only a touch of flavour, but I prefer to leave them in. Add the wine, salt and pepper, and simmer, covered, for about 30 minutes or until the chicken is very tender. Serve hot.

CLAUDIA RODEN

Thai barbecued pork

Serves 6
2 pork fillets

For the marinade
2 tbsp clear honey
2 tbsp light oil
2 tbsp dry sherry
1 tbsp ginger juice (*see* p. 130)
1 tsp salt
1 tbsp sugar
2 cloves garlic, crushed

Mix together the marinade ingredients and marinate the meat in it for at least 2 hours. Grill the meat for 20–25 minutes, turning it over once and brushing occasionally with the marinade until it is well done and well browned.

Serve, cut in slices, accompanied by sliced tomatoes, cucumber, pineapple and spring onions cut in half lengthways, and plain rice.

The meat may also be cooked on the barbecue.

CLAUDIA RODEN

Tunisian lamb stew with lemon and turmeric

This recipe was given to Claudia Roden by two Tunisian brothers, Ben and Kamel Tilouche, who run a restaurant in London.

Serves 6

4 tbsp olive or vegetable oil
900g/2lb shoulder or leg of lamb,
trimmed of fat and cut into pieces
6 cloves garlic, peeled
1½ lemons, peeled and sliced
1½ tsp turmeric
salt and pepper
675g/1½lb small waxy potatoes, peeled

Heat the oil in a large saucepan and brown the meat. Add the garlic, lemon slices, turmeric, salt and pepper, and enough water to cover. Simmer very gently, with the lid on, for 1 hour or until the meat is tender, adding extra water if necessary. Add the potatoes and more water if necessary and continue to cook, covered, until the potatoes are done, a further 15 minutes or so.   CLAUDIA RODEN

Editor's note: The lemon disintegrates during cooking, amalgamating with the garlic and turmeric in a way which is full of savour yet delightfully refreshing. If more convenient, the stew may be cooked in advance, and the potatoes added when you come to reheat and eat the dish.

Texmex tacos with spiced beef filling and tomato and chilli salsa

This dish from Thane Prince is great fun to eat. It reflects the growing popularity of the cooking of the American Deep South – as does the nifty Creole seasoning that follows.

Serves 4

450g/1lb lean minced beef
1 large clove garlic, chopped
1 tsp ground cumin
1 tsp dried oregano
$^1/_4$ tsp cayenne pepper, or to taste
3 tsp sweet paprika
400g/14oz tinned tomatoes
425g/15oz tinned red kidney beans, drained
salt and black pepper to taste
8–12 taco shells

Cook the meat in a large saucepan, stirring over a medium heat until the fat runs. Add the garlic and continue to cook until the meat is well browned. Add all the seasonings and stir-fry these with the meat for 1 minute. Meanwhile, put the tomatoes and beans in a blender or food processor and blend briefly until they are chopped. Add this mixture to the spiced meat and stir, scraping up any spices that may have stuck to the pan. Season to taste, bring to the boil, cover and simmer over a low heat for 30 minutes. The mixture will become very thick, so stir occasionally, adding a little water if necessary to prevent it sticking to the pan.

To serve the tacos: heat the taco shells for 15 minutes in a medium oven allowing 2–3 per person. In separate dishes, have ready some shredded crisp lettuce, chopped ripe tomatoes, grated Cheddar cheese and chopped Spanish onion. Each person takes a warm shell and adds fillings as they like, topping the completed taco with a little of the piquant salsa below.

Fresh tomato and chilli salsa

450g/1lb fresh ripe tomatoes
1 small green chilli, washed, de-seeded and finely chopped (wash your hands well after touching the chillis)
1/2 medium onion, finely chopped
1–2 tbsp chopped parsley
1 tbsp fresh lime or lemon juice
salt and pepper

Peel the tomatoes by plunging into boiling water for 60 seconds and then remove the skins. Chop and put into a serving bowl. Add all the other ingredients and stir, seasoning to taste.

THANE PRINCE

Simone Sekers writes: TORTILLA/TACO: The tortilla is a Mexican pancake made of flour which is ground from cooked corn. When tortillas are fried until crisp, they become tacos. Taco 'shells' are available in most supermarkets and delicatessens, but tortillas are more elusive. Indian chapattis, which are often easier to obtain, can be used instead.

Creole seasoning

This pungent spice, writes Thane Prince, can be used in many ways to season white fish, salmon, chicken or pork steaks. To use, wash the meat or fish and pat dry, leaving a little moisture on the surface so that the spices will adhere. Using about 1 tsp of spice per portion, coat the meat or fish on all sides and leave to absorb the flavours for 30 minutes. To cook, heat a mixture of butter and oil in a frying pan and pan-fry the meat or fish on all sides until the surface has a rich dark brown crust and the flesh is cooked through. A rich sauce can be made by stirring a pint of cream into the pan juices. For lovers of grilled food, brush the seasoned fish or meat with a little oil and grill in the usual manner.

2 tbsp dried onion flakes
1 tbsp fennel seeds
1 tbsp dried thyme
1 tbsp dried sage
1 tsp cumin
2 tbsp garlic salt
2 tsp paprika
1 tsp black pepper
1 tsp cayenne pepper, or to taste

Place the onion flakes and whole herbs and spices in a coffee grinder and whizz until powdered. Mix with the ready-ground spices and store until needed.

THANE PRINCE

LONG SLOW MEAT COOKERY

Aromatic meat dishes are some of the best dishes it is possible to make. Rich in savour and full of flavour, they fill the kitchen with good smells and can be left to cook themselves. I think of them as the savoury equivalent of a traditional English pudding. Comforting food *par excellence*, they engender a feeling of immense satisfaction and well-being; I know of no one who does not enjoy eating them. For a busy cook they are ideal: they require but a few minutes' preparation, and many are better for being made in advance and reheated one or two days later.

These dishes also make the very best of cheaper cuts of meat which, though tougher, are sweeter and have more flavour than many prime cuts. Long slow cooking renders them tender as butter, and yields wonderfully dense-flavoured sauces. Success depends merely on cooking them gently – an Aga is ideal for this. It is also important to make sure they are well sealed. Insert a sheet of greaseproof paper between the casserole dish and lid, which forms a much better seal, I have found, than aluminium foil. In the absence of an Aga, leaving the meat to cool in the turned-off oven has a marvellously mellowing effect on the dish, and is a practice I now customarily follow.

Potato flour, or *fécule*, is a useful thickener for this type of dish (see Simone Sekers' notes which follow). It is tasteless and needs no cooking out – simply mix it with a little water, adding it gradually, a teaspoon at a time, to the casserole or sauce, stirring constantly over a gentle heat until the desired thickness is reached, usually just enough to cohere and bind the sauce lightly.

Simone Sekers writes: POTATO FLOUR is made by soaking pulped potatoes in water and collecting the starch which sinks to the bottom, and then drying it. It is ideal for those on a gluten-free diet, and is one of the best thickening agents for sauces and stews, since it produces a much lighter texture than wheat flour, needs no extra fat to help it blend, and will thicken a dish after only the gentlest of simmers (do not boil the liquid vigorously afterwards or it will thin again). Mix it with a little of the liquid before adding it to the rest. It is worth buying when in France (look for *fécule*, rather than *farine*), where it is as basic a product as cornflour is in this country. Here, it can be found in good grocers, delicatessens and wholefood shops.

Braised and roasted shoulder of lamb with haricot beans

Shoulder of lamb is a particularly sweet and luscious meat, but inclined to be fatty. This method of cooking it – a gentle braise to tenderise the meat (which can be done the previous day) followed by a hot blast in the oven – is quite the best I know, removing much of the fat while rendering the joint both meltingly tender and well crisped. In this recipe, beans are cooked along with the meat, but you can easily adapt the recipe to other ingredients, cooking the meat, for example, on a bed of potatoes or a mixture of onions and quinces, adding wine or brandy and other aromatics such as garlic and thyme.

Serves 4–6

1 whole shoulder of lamb, approx. 2kg/4½lb, trimmed
of obvious fat
170g/6oz haricot beans, soaked overnight in water, and
cooked in fresh water for 15–20 minutes
2 ripe quartered tomatoes
2 chopped anchovy fillets
1 tsp potato flour slaked in little water

Drain the parcooked beans and spread them out in the bottom of a flame-proof casserole dish big enough to take the shoulder of lamb. Distribute the tomatoes and anchovies on top and pour in enough water to cover the beans. Brown the lamb on both sides as best you can in a non-stick frying pan, then place on top of the beans. Bring to the boil, cover tightly, transfer to a low oven, 140°C/275°F/gas mark 1, and cook for about 1¼ hours until the meat is beginning to shrink away from the bone. Turn off the heat and leave the casserole in the turned-off oven for at least an hour or until the oven has cooled.

For the final cooking, remove the joint, score the skin in diamond fashion and set on a trivet over a roasting pan. Cook in a hot oven, 200°C/400°F/gas mark 6, for around 50 minutes, or until well browned and crisp – a little longer will do no harm.

Meanwhile, using a piece of absorbent kitchen paper, mop up the surface fat from the remaining liquid and beans in the casserole (if the fat has set this can be picked off with a spoon). Remove the beans and set aside. Set the casserole over a low heat and let the liquid reduce to around 150–240ml/5–8fl. oz, by which time it will be richly flavoured, skimming as necessary. Thicken with the potato flour as described above and reheat the beans in the sauce.

Set the lamb on a serving dish and serve hot, straight from the oven, carving it into thick slices or chunks on to hot plates, handing the beans round separately. A few new potatoes, or baked potatoes, go well with this dish.

LYNDA BROWN

Provençale shin of beef with wine and brandy

Shin of beef is another greatly undervalued cut of meat, with little fat, no waste, and an excellent flavour. Long slow cooking breaks down the connective tissues present to yield gelatine-rich gravy, the mark of distinction of all truly good French *daubes*. The orange rind, garlic and pork rind (or a split trotter) are characteristic of the *daubes* of Provence, but can be left out if preferred – though I always include a strip of pork rind for the enriching quality it imparts to all of these dishes.

Serves 4

4 large thick slices of shin of beef
1 tbsp beef fat or olive oil for frying
55ml/2fl. oz brandy or Armagnac
300ml/10fl. oz red wine; or use half wine,
half beef stock
large sprig of thyme

plus, optionally
thin strip of scrubbed orange rind
clove of garlic, crushed
strip of pork rind

To finish
1–2 tsp potato flour (see p. 39), slaked in a little water
fried carrots or mushrooms as garnish

Seal the meat on both sides in the fat or oil over a fairly high heat in a non-stick pan until well browned. Lower the heat, pour in the brandy and ignite (stand well back), shaking the pan to ensure that the alcohol is burned off. Add the wine or wine and stock, and cook for 3–4 minutes. Transfer everything to a heavy ovenproof casserole dish. Tuck the thyme and other seasonings, if used, down into the liquid, cover very tightly and cook in the lowest possible oven, around 130°C/250°F/gas mark 1/2, for 3–31/2 hours until the meat is tender. Leave the dish in the turned-off oven until cool, and keep until the following day, or even a day later if it suits you.

41

Reheat gently on top of the stove. Discard the seasonings and arrange the meat in a serving dish. Bind the sauce, which by now should be dark and rich, with the potato flour as described on p. 39 to give the desired thickness, and pour over the meat.

Garnish round with either batons of carrots well browned in a little butter and olive oil, or fried mushrooms stewed gently with some finely chopped garlic and parsley for about 10 minutes, finished with 1 tbsp of brandy swilled around the pan at the last minute. Serve with pasta.

LYNDA BROWN

Sticky braised oxtail with wine and carrots

Oxtail is probably the most underrated cut of meat you can buy. Nothing produces such wonderfully lip-smacking, rib-sticking winter braises, best made one day and served the next.

Serves 4

8 large pieces of oxtail, approx. 1.5kg/3¹/₂lb, trimmed of all fat (buy two whole oxtail, saving the small bits for soup)

For the marinade
150ml/5fl. oz each of red wine and port; or 300ml/
10fl. oz red wine
1 onion, sliced
2 large carrots, peeled and cut into wedges

For the cooking
1 large sprig of thyme
1 piece of scrubbed orange peel
1 strip of pork rind
600ml/1pt beef stock or water

Put the oxtail in a large bowl with the marinade ingredients and leave in a cool place for 6–8 hours, turning the meat occasionally.

Transfer everything to a heavy ovenproof casserole, tucking in the thyme, orange peel and pork rind. Pour on the stock or water and bring gently to the boil. Cover very tightly (placing a piece of greaseproof paper between dish and lid) and cook in a very low oven, 130–140°C/250–275°F/gas mark

1/2–1, for 3 hours. The liquid should barely tremble – adjust the oven temperature accordingly. Leave the meat to cool in the turned-off oven, then refrigerate overnight.

Next day, remove the surface fat. Heat the jellied sauce until it melts, then take out the pieces of meat and carrots, transferring them to a large, shallow ovenproof dish which will take the meat in a single layer. Strain the sauce into a clean pan and reduce by about a quarter, skimming often. Pour over the meat (it should come no more than three-quarters of the way up the meat). Cook for 45–60 minutes in a hot oven, 200°C/400°F/gas mark 6, basting occasionally and turning the meat halfway through, until the oxtail has become glazed and the sauce has darkened and become deliciously rich. Thicken slightly if necessary. Serve with plain mashed potato and crisply cooked cabbage.

Variations: Lightly caramelised pickling onions are excellent with this dish: allow 450g/1lb for 4, boil them, unpeeled, for 3–4 minutes with water to cover, drain, then slip off the skins which will now peel off easily. Cook gently with a little butter in a covered pan until soft, adding 1–2 tsp sugar towards the end. Arrange around the oxtail and serve.

Sometimes I include prunes with the oxtail, which add an extra richness. Allow 3–4 per person and soak them for 2 days beforehand (the prune liquor can go into the sauce), or use the quick prunes in brandy on p. 240. Add the prunes about halfway through the second stage, when you give the oxtail the final cooking in a hot oven, so that they have time to become plump and very hot. This time, serve with pasta, polenta or rice.

LYNDA BROWN

Beef braised with fresh peas

This summer braise is the kind of dish you can do anywhere, any time and which anyone can cook. Don't stint on the peas – they acquire a lovely meaty flavour which enhances their sweetness perfectly.

Serves 4–6

1.125–1.5kg/2¹/₂–3lb joint of topside or silverside
30–55g/1–2oz butter
1 tsp oil
675–900g/1¹/₂–2lb fresh peas, shelled weight

Choose a heavy casserole dish which will just take the meat comfortably. Heat a little butter, adding a tsp of oil to prevent the butter from burning, and seal the meat on all sides. Fill all the space around with fresh peas. Put extra dabs of butter on top and cover tightly (inserting a piece of greaseproof paper between dish and lid). Pot roast for 3–3$\frac{1}{2}$ hours at 140–150°C/275–300°F/gas mark 1–2, checking halfway through that the meat is cooking gently, adjusting the oven temperature accordingly.

The beef and peas produce their own delicious gravy. Carve in thick slices, and serve with potatoes and horseradish sauce.

LYNDA BROWN

GUY FAWKES' NIGHT

Guy Fawkes' Night may not be what it used to be when I was a child, but the pleasure of standing in front of a bonfire on a cold night, hands cupped around a mug of warming soup, or eating baked potatoes with the butter dribbling down your chin, never diminishes. Here are a few dishes (and drinks) for outdoor hardy types, and winter picnics.

Madhur Jaffrey's chicken mulligatawny soup

Serves 6–8

170g/6oz red lentils
1 medium potato, peeled and cubed
1.2l/2pt chicken stock
½ tsp turmeric
200g/7oz raw chicken breast meat
salt and pepper
5 cloves garlic, finely chopped
3.75cm/1½in piece of fresh ginger, peeled and finely chopped
1 heaped tsp ground cumin
1 heaped tsp coriander
¼ tsp cayenne pepper
2 tbsp vegetable oil
240ml/8fl. oz water
1 tbsp lemon juice
1 tbsp mango chutney (optional)

This is a slight adaptation of the original recipe which has become a family favourite. Put the lentils, potato, chicken stock and turmeric into a heavy saucepan, bring to the boil, cover and simmer until the lentils and potato are soft, 30–40 minutes. Purée in a blender.

Meanwhile, chop the chicken finely, mix with ¼ tsp salt and some black pepper and leave to stand. Gently fry the garlic, ginger, cumin, coriander and cayenne pepper in the oil in the cleaned pan, stirring well, until the mixture browns slightly. Add the chopped chicken and fry until it becomes opaque. Add the water and simmer until the chicken is cooked, about 3–4 minutes. Return the puréed soup to the pan and add lemon juice, mango chutney if using, and salt to taste. Cook for a further 3–4 minutes for the flavours to blend. Serve hot.

THANE PRINCE

Pumpkin muffins (v)

These can be made in advance and reheated.

Makes 18

285g/10oz wholemeal flour
110g/4oz soft brown sugar
1 tbsp baking powder
2 tsp cinnamon
1 tsp freshly grated nutmeg
1/4 tsp salt
1 egg
60ml/2fl. oz corn oil
approx. 180ml/6fl. oz milk
225g/8oz pumpkin flesh, finely grated
55g/2oz raisins
55g/2oz chopped walnuts

Mix the flour, sugar, baking powder, spices and salt in a roomy bowl. Beat the egg with the oil in a measuring jug and add sufficient milk to make 300ml/10fl. oz liquid. Add the oil/milk mixture to the flour mixture, followed by the pumpkin, raisins and walnuts. Mix just well enough to make sure everything is combined; the muffins will be chewy if the ingredients are overmixed. Line 18 deep bun tins with paper cases and divide the mixture between them; the cases will be almost full. Bake in a preheated oven, 190°C/375°F/gas mark 5, for 30–40 minutes until the muffins are browned and a skewer inserted into the centre of a muffin comes out clean. Serve hot.

THANE PRINCE

Grilled sausages with spiced green lentils

Serves 4–6

675g/1½lb good pork or venison sausages, grilled

For the spiced lentils
1 shallot, chopped
1 tbsp oil
1 tsp cumin seeds
170g/6oz green lentils, washed
600ml/1pt water
salt and pepper
1 large or 2 medium tomatoes, peeled and chopped

To finish
1 medium onion, finely sliced
2 plump cloves of garlic, sliced
1 tbsp oil

For the spiced lentils, fry the shallot in the oil until it begins to colour. Add the cumin seeds and stir-fry for 30 seconds. Put in the lentils, add the water, bring to the boil and simmer, covered, until tender, about 50 minutes. Season to taste with salt and pepper, add the tomato and simmer, uncovered, for a further 5–10 minutes.

In a frying pan, fry the onion and garlic in oil until crisp and golden. Put the lentils into a hot serving dish and pour over the onion, garlic and oil mixture. Serve with the sausages.

THANE PRINCE

Moroccan meat pies

These fragrantly spiced meat pastries from Claudia Roden make a change from the usual fillings and are splendid cold-weather food.

Serves 4

2 onions, chopped
3 tbsp oil
450g/1lb minced lamb or beef
3 tsp ground cinnamon
pinch of cayenne pepper (optional)
salt and pepper
bunch of parsley, finely chopped
bunch of coriander, finely chopped
6 eggs, beaten
450g/1lb puff pastry
plain flour
oil for deep frying

Fry the onions in the oil until golden. Add the meat, 1¹/₂ tsp of the cinnamon, a pinch of cayenne pepper if liked, salt and pepper, and fry, stirring occasionally, until the meat becomes dry. Add the parsley and coriander and stir in the eggs. Keep stirring and cook for a minute or so until the eggs are set.

Cut the pastry into eight pieces. Make little balls and roll out on a floured surface as thinly as possible without breaking, using a floured rolling pin. Place 2 heaped tbsp of filling on one side near the centre of each sheet and fold into a packet. Pinch the edges together so as to close the pies firmly. Deep-fry in batches in not-too-hot oil until well browned, about 5 minutes, turning once. Drain on absorbent paper and serve very hot, sprinkled with the remaining cinnamon.

CLAUDIA RODEN

Iranian meat omelette

Serves 4–6

1 large onion, finely chopped
1 leek or a few spring onions, finely chopped
butter for frying
450g/1lb minced beef or lamb
110g/4oz spinach, fresh or frozen
1 sprig parsley, finely chopped
1 tsp cinnamon or allspice
salt and pepper
6 eggs, lightly beaten

Fry the onion and leek or spring onion in a little butter until soft. Add the meat and fry until it has changed colour. Add the spinach, parsley and cinnamon or allspice, salt and pepper. Stir well then combine with the beaten eggs in a bowl. Melt a knob of butter in a non-stick frying pan. When it is hot, pour in the mixture and cook slowly over a gentle heat for about 15 minutes. Turn the omelette over (with the help of a plate or lid), or put it under the grill for a minute or so to brown the top. This can be eaten hot or cold. CLAUDIA RODEN

See also: Barbecued vegetables and fruit, pp. 135–6 and 138.

MULLED drinks are just the thing for cold weather, cold houses, and cold winters. Here are two suggestions from Thane Prince.

Mulled cider with honey and rum

Makes 8 large glasses

1l/1³/4pt cider
1 sherry glass of dark rum, or to taste
1 tbsp honey, or to taste
2 blades mace
1 10cm/4in cinnamon stick
1 orange, sliced
1 eating apple, cored and sliced

Mix all the ingredients in a large pan, stirring gently. Do not allow to boil. Serve in heavy glasses or china mugs. THANE PRINCE

Virginia non-alcoholic fruit cup

Makes 10–12 glasses

1.2l/2pt apple juice
300ml/10fl. oz each of orange and pineapple juice
150ml/5fl. oz lemon juice
1 stick cinnamon
5 cloves
sugar to taste

Put all the ingredients into a large pan, simmer for a few minutes and serve.

THANE PRINCE

DESSERTS

Sweet liqueur soufflé

Serves 4

2 large egg yolks
2 tbsp caster sugar
90ml/3fl. oz Grand Marnier or Chartreuse
4 large egg whites

Butter a large flat ovenproof serving dish. Using an electric whisk, cream the egg yolks and half the sugar in a bowl until pale and thick. Add the liqueur and briefly whisk again. In another bowl, whisk the egg whites to a soft snow, then add the rest of the sugar and continue whisking until the mixture is stiff and shiny. Very lightly fold the two mixtures together – don't worry about lumps of egg white. Pile on to the dish, sprinkle sparingly with extra sugar and bake at 200°C/400°F/gas mark 6 for 9–10 minutes: it is ready when well risen and lightly browned. Inside, it will be moist and just comfortably warm. Serve immediately, hot plates at the ready.

Variation: Slices of fresh fruit – strawberries, peaches, cherries, mango – can be scattered over the base first, and the soufflé mixture spooned on top.

LYNDA BROWN

Hot chocolate and almond soufflé

Serves 4–6

4 large eggs, separated
110g/4oz plain chocolate
55g/2oz ground almonds
2 tbsp brandy
single cream for serving
butter for greasing
3 tbsp caster sugar, plus extra for sprinkling

Have ready a well-buttered soufflé or straight-sided dish about 17.5cm/7in across, and sprinkle the inside with caster sugar. Using an electric whisk, beat the egg yolks with the sugar until you have a pale light mousse. Melt the chocolate in a bowl over a pan of hot water and reserve. Beat the egg whites until stiff but not dry. Fold the almonds, brandy and melted chocolate into the mousse, then carefully fold in the egg whites. Pour into the prepared dish and bake in a preheated hot oven, 200°C/400°F/gas mark 6, for 20–25 minutes. The soufflé will be soft in the middle. Serve hot with a little single cream.

THANE PRINCE

Editor's note: This is a rich soufflé, and small portions are sufficient. Chocolate can be tricky to melt if overheated, as it will 'scramble' and harden. The melted chocolate should be barely warm and should be melted very slowly, in a thick basin, set over hot (not boiling) water. Make sure the water does not touch the bottom of the basin. Break the chocolate up into small pieces, let it melt undisturbed (about 10 minutes), take away from the heat, stir gently and fold into the soufflé as described above.

Strawberry and almond tart

Strawberries and almonds are a classic combination. This tart, from Thane Prince, is a good picnic dessert also. She advises that the basic tart may be baked the day before but not filled with the strawberries nor glazed until the day it is to be eaten.

Serves 6–8

23cm/9in flan dish lined with 225g/8oz sweet
shortcrust pastry

For the filling
100g/3¹/₂oz blanched almonds,
100g/3¹/₂oz butter
100g/3¹/₂oz caster sugar
1 whole egg, plus 1 egg yolk
1 tbsp plain flour
1 tbsp almond liqueur (optional)

To finish
675g/1¹/₂lb strawberries, cleaned and hulled
4 tbsp apple or redcurrant jelly for glazing

Place the almonds in a food processor and process until finely ground. Add the eggs, flour and liqueur (if using) and process again to mix well.

Pour this frangipane mixture into the prepared pastry shell and bake in a preheated moderate oven, 180°C/350°F/gas mark 4, for 20–25 minutes until golden brown. Remove from the oven and allow to cool.

To assemble, carefully place the strawberries, pointed end up, on the tart in circles, starting at the outside and continuing until the pie is covered. Thin the jelly with 1 tbsp water and boil for 1 minute, allow to cool and then brush over the berries.

THANE PRINCE

Editor's note: Blanched almonds have a better flavour than ready ground almonds and produce a more attractive slightly gritty texture when ground in a food processor.

Nieve de mango sorbet

Serves 4

4 ripe mangoes
juice of 1/2–1 lime
1–2 tbsp dark rum (optional)
5 or more tbsp sugar (optional)
210ml/7fl. oz water

Peel the mangoes and blend the flesh with the lime and rum according to taste. Add sugar if necessary, if the mangoes are very sweet, you may not need it. Add the water and blend to a light purée. Pour into an ice-cube tray, cover with cling film or foil, and put in the freezer for a few hours until hard. Just before serving, blend a few cubes at a time to a fine cream in a food processor.

CLAUDIA RODEN

See also: Passion fruit sorbet, p. 29; Majorcan ice cream, p. 148; Apricot ice, p. 209.

Chocolate chip ice-cream

No cookery book is complete without at least one ice-cream. Here is the finger-lickin', all-time American favourite from Thane Prince, 'made even more special if you have both the time and the inclination to hand-chop the chips'.

Serves 4

For the custard
300ml/10fl. oz milk
3 egg yolks
85g/3oz caster sugar
1 tbsp cornflour mixed with 3 tbsp milk
300ml/10fl. oz double cream
1 tsp vanilla essence

To finish
110g/4oz plain chocolate or chocolate chips

Bring the milk to the boil in a heavy saucepan. In a bowl, beat the yolks with the sugar until thick and light. Pour on the hot milk, then pour this mixture on to the slaked cornflour and return everything to the pan. Stirring constantly, heat the custard gently until it begins to thicken. Allow the surface to bubble for about 60 seconds to cook the cornflour, then remove from the heat, cover the surface of the custard with a circle of greased paper and leave to cool.

Beat the cream until floppy and mix this and the vanilla essence into the cooled custard. Either place in an ice-cream maker and freeze according to the manufacturer's instructions, or place in a deep container in the coldest part of the freezer. If freezing this way you will need to beat out the ice crystals two or three times. Just before the ice-cream is solid, stir in the chocolate chips. Store in the freezer and remove to the refrigerator for 20 minutes before serving. THANE PRINCE

Konafa with cheese

This is something of an indulgence, for the simple reason that, outside London, *konafa* (see Simone Sekers, below) is very difficult to find. But I couldn't resist it. As Claudia Roden wrote in *Mediterranean Cookery*, where the recipe was also published, this, the Arab version of the more familiar Greek and Turkish pastries on sale here, is one of the best Arab desserts: 'Eat it hot from the oven, first pouring the cold syrup through the crisp sizzling pastry into the bland cream cheese. Forget the commercial pastries of the same name and make your own – an entirely different experience.' So, badger your delicatessen or save it up for your next foraging trip to London.

Serves 10 or more

450g/1lb *konafa*
225g/8oz unsalted butter, melted
900g/2lb ricotta (*see* p. 210)

For the syrup
450g/1lb sugar
300ml/10fl. oz water
1 tbsp lemon juice
2 tbsp orange-flower water or rose-water or both

To finish
85g/3oz pistachio nuts, finely chopped

Preheat the oven to 180°C/350°F/gas mark 4. Put the raw *konafa* into a large bowl, then pour the melted and slightly cooled butter over it. Pull out and separate the strands and mix them well with your hands so that they do not stick together and are all thoroughly coated with butter.

Spread out half the pastry evenly in the bottom of a large round baking tray or ovenproof dish, crumble the ricotta evenly over it and cover with a layer of the remaining pastry. Press down firmly with your hands so that it all holds together compactly. Bake for 45 minutes, then turn up the oven to 230°C/450°F/gas mark 8 and bake for 15 minutes longer, or until it is light golden.

Prepare the syrup as soon as you put the pastry in the oven, so that it has time to cool. Boil the sugar and water with the lemon juice for about 15 minutes or until it is thick enough to coat the back of a spoon, then add the orange flower water and/or rose-water. Simmer for 30 seconds longer, let it cool, then put it in the refrigerator to chill.

When the pastry is cooked, immediately cut round it with a sharp knife and turn out on to a large round serving plate. Pour over the syrup and sprinkle with pistachios. You could also serve it from the tray and use less syrup – even half the quantity if you prefer.

CLAUDIA RODEN

Simone Sekers writes: KONAFA (also called *kadaif*) is soft, white vermicelli or shredded-wheat-like strands of briefly cooked dough, and is available from Greek and Cypriot grocers and some oriental stores. Like filo pastry it is made with flour and water (which is why copious quantities of butter are usually added later), in this case by pouring the batter through a sieve set over a hot plate which sets the dough immediately; it is then scooped up ready to be used. It can be frozen, but should be wrapped well first and taken out of the bag to defrost.

Grilled goat's cheese in vine leaves Ⓥ

For each person you need one vine leaf and a 30–45g/1–1½oz portion of soft or semi-soft goat's cheese. Lightly brush both sides of the vine leaf with olive oil. Form the cheese into a round and fold up in the vine leaf. Place on a heatproof dish and grill until the top of the vine leaf begins to blacken. Serve immediately with a fresh apricot sauce made by stewing chopped apricots with vanilla sugar to taste in a little water for 5–8 minutes until soft, and accompany with a glass of chilled Jurançon wine.

Note: These may also be served as a first course with olives, a few salad leaves and chopped ripe tomatoes mixed with a little vinaigrette.

LYNDA BROWN

Simone Sekers writes: VINE LEAVES are usually sold preserved in brine, which should be rinsed off and the leaves patted dry on paper towels before using. If you have a supply of fresh vine leaves from a nearby vine, choose those which are fully grown but still young and supple (June–July is the best time to pick them), and blanch them momentarily in boiling salted water – just long enough for them to become flexible. Any surplus can be frozen. Wrap them in handy quantities in foil or plastic bags. Their unique, tart lemony flavour is not to be found in any other large, stuffable leaf, but you can sometimes just get away with the large leaves of spinach beet, if you add plenty of extra lemon juice to the recipe.

A Feast of Fish

FISH HAS NEVER been more popular. Low in saturated fat, high in protein and easy to prepare, it is an ideal choice in a healthy diet. And now that fatty fish such as herrings, mackerel, tuna and salmon have been found to be of particular benefit in helping to reduce the risk of heart attack, fish is in the spotlight as never before. Fishmongers and supermarkets have also played their part and now offer a far wider choice than just the traditional varieties of cod, haddock, whiting and plaice. Today, exotic fish of all kinds appears on fishmongers' slabs and squid, tuna, monkfish, bream and red mullet have become commonplace.

As our appetite for fish increases, so we are becoming more adventurous in the ways we cook it. Fish is very adaptable and offers tremendous scope in this respect. Cod, for example, is as marvellous cooked with oriental spices as it is with a robust tomato sauce, or garlic and olive oil, or in the time-honoured way with mashed potatoes. Often, too, one type of fish can be substituted for another, and all fish can be cooked in a wide variety of ways, hot or cold, as a main dish, in soups, salads, or as an appetiser.

Fish cookery is also one of the most rewarding aspects of modern cooking, for it enables the cook to produce healthy, interesting dishes with very little effort. It is with these thoughts in mind that I have selected the recipes for this chapter, choosing dishes from across the world as well as a few modern ideas from Thane Prince and one or two old favourites such as a very superior fish pie, which, done well, is still one of the most glorious fish dishes ever invented.

Though not yet a luxury, fish is no longer cheap. It is more perishable than meat, and good kitchen practice is essential to keep fish at its freshest. Wherever practical, get your fish home as quickly as possible (leave it with the fishmonger until you are ready to go home, rather than in a warm car). Once home, remove it from the bag immediately, wipe with kitchen paper, and keep packed between ice cubes in a shallow bowl covered in cling film (or between two plates) in the refrigerator. If you want to keep the fish for 24 hours (which is fine for decent fresh fish), ask the fishmonger to remove the heads and guts. Wash out all the blood, pat dry, and keep as above.

Tomato, mussel and saffron soup

One of the easiest and best fish soups I know.

Serves 4–6

675g/1½lb/1½pt mussels
675g/1½lb ripe tomatoes, coarsely chopped
1 small onion/2 shallots/white part of 1 leek,
finely chopped
1 tbsp chopped parsley
approx. 150ml/5fl. oz white wine or water

To finish
½–1 packet (0.125 grains) powdered saffron (*see* p. 69)
up to 150ml/5fl. oz single cream
1–2 tsp potato flour (*see* p. 39)
little extra finely chopped parsley

Have your mussels scrubbed and prepared in the usual way, discarding any which do not close when tapped sharply with a knife. Put into a large pan with the tomatoes, onion and parsley and enough wine or water to moisten the bottom. Cover with a tight-fitting lid, bring to the boil and simmer for 5 minutes. Discard any mussels still unopened.

Meanwhile, dissolve the powdered saffron in a little of the cream. Stir 1 tsp of potato flour into this and mix into the chowder, adding extra cream to taste. Bring to the boil, scatter with parsley, pour into a large tureen or large soup plates and serve immediately, with good bread to mop up the delicious sauce.

Note: The potato flour serves to bind and cohere the sauce, which should be only slightly thickened. If sauce is still runny, add the second teaspoon, slaked with the cream as before.

LYNDA BROWN

Simone Sekers writes: MUSSELS are essentially a cold-weather treat, in season from September to April, and one of the cheapest and most versatile of all the shellfish. They are always sold live and are best eaten on the day you buy them. If you do have to keep them until the next day, put them into a bucket of water to which you have added a handful of salt. Sprinkle the surface with bran or oatmeal, so that the mussels use this to get rid of any sand or grit. When preparing them check that each shell is tightly closed, or that, if open, it closes quickly when tapped. Discard any which remain open. Remove the 'beard' with a quick tug, scrub the shells well, and rinse under cold running water. Also available, although less widely, are the very large, green-lipped mussels, which have a distinctive iridescent bright green edge to the open shell – they make a good addition to a fishy first course, and to paella.

Haddock, prawn and sweetcorn chowder

Serves 5–6

2 medium leeks, cleaned and sliced
3 medium potatoes, peeled and cubed
2 tbsp oil
850ml/1½pt water
½ tsp salt
140g/5oz sweetcorn kernels, fresh or frozen, or
drained tinned corn
225g/8oz haddock or similar white fish (skinned, boned
weight), cut into 2.5cm/1in cubes
110g/4oz prawns (shelled weight)
3 medium tomatoes, peeled and chopped
salt and black pepper
2 tbsp chopped fresh parsley

In a large pan, sweat the leek and potato in the oil for 2–3 minutes. Do not brown. Add the water and salt, bring to the boil and simmer for 15–20 minutes or until the potatoes are soft. Using a potato masher, mash the vegetables roughly. Meanwhile, if using fresh or frozen corn, simmer for 5 minutes in 300ml/10fl. oz water and reserve. Add the fish to the soup. Simmer for 2–3 minutes (the fish cooks very quickly), then add the prawns, tomatoes and the corn with its cooking liquid or 300ml/10fl. oz extra water if using tinned corn. Continue to cook the soup very gently until everything is heated through, taste to correct the seasoning and stir in the chopped parsley.

THANE PRINCE

Prawns in Provençale sauce

For this recipe, writes Claudia Roden, it is better to use unpeeled prawns and peel them yourself.

Serves 4

900g/2lb unpeeled prawns, or 340g/12oz peeled
cooked prawns

For the Provençale sauce
1 onion, finely chopped
2 tbsp olive oil
2 garlic cloves, finely chopped
675g/1½lb ripe tomatoes, peeled and chopped
1 small hot chilli pepper, seeds removed and
finely chopped (optional)
3 tbsp cognac
150ml/5fl. oz dry white wine
1 tsp thyme
1 bay leaf
pinch of cayenne pepper
salt and pepper

To finish
large bunch of parsley, finely chopped

Peel the prawns if necessary. Fry the onion in the olive oil until golden. Add the garlic and fry until its aroma rises. Add the tomatoes and the remaining ingredients except the prawns. Simmer, uncovered, for about 20 minutes or until the sauce is a rich aromatic purée.

Add the prawns and heat through for 1–2 minutes until hot (or until the prawns are cooked if using fresh prawns). Serve immediately, with good bread, garnished with plenty of parsley.

CLAUDIA RODEN

Scallop and broad bean salad, with tomato vinaigrette

Scallops are a good choice for *salades tièdes* (*see* p.156). They require no preparation to speak of, cook quickly, and have a lovely sea-fresh taste and moist
flesh. If you want to use the larger and more expensive scallops, allow 2 per
person, slicing each horizontally in half and cooking the coral separately.

Serves 4

170g/6oz young broad beans
340g/12oz Queenie scallops, washed, and any dark
veins removed
selection of salad leaves, washed, dried and arranged
on 4 separate plates

For the dressing
1 large ripe tomato, peeled and de-seeded, chopped
to a pulp
1/2 tsp sugar
1 dsp sherry or good-quality wine vinegar
pinch of salt
2 tbsp olive oil, plus 4 tsp for dribbling over the salad
leaves

Cook the beans in a little water until tender, 3 4 minutes, then remove the
skins and keep hot. Steam the scallops between two plates set over boiling water for about 5 minutes, turning once, until just cooked.
Meanwhile, mix all the ingredients for the fresh tomato vinaigrette and
warm through gently. Dribble 1 tsp of olive oil over each plate of waiting
salad leaves. Arrange the scallops and broad beans on top, spoon over
the warmed vinaigrette and serve immediately as a first course.

LYNDA BROWN

Salade tahitienne

Coconut milk is one of the best flavourings I know for fish, either used as
a marinade, as here, or in soups (*see* p. 64), or used to bake fish with other
flavourings such as ginger, chilli, coriander and cumin. Tinned coconut
milk is adequate for this dish but fresh is better. This salad, included in
one of Claudia Roden's articles, comes from the celebrated Australian

chef Stephanie Alexander, who has her own restaurant in Melbourne. Scallops are also good for this dish.

Serves 4

450g/1lb very fresh, firm, white fish fillets, skinned
(choose any favourite sweet variety of fish)
juice of 2 limes or 1 lemon
120ml/4fl. oz coconut milk (*see* p. 64)
¹/₂ red pepper, cut into small dice
¹/₂ green pepper, cut into small dice
1 ripe medium tomato, skinned, de-seeded and
cut into dice
¹/₂ small red onion, cut into paper-thin rings

Cut the fish into cubes or thin slices. Put into a glass bowl and pour over the citrus juice. Cover and chill for a minimum of 3 hours, and no more than 8, turning the fish after an hour. When the fish is quite opaque, drain through a colander, pressing gently to extract as much of the juice as possible. Discard this liquid. Spoon the coconut milk over the fish and reserve. Arrange the peppers and tomato as a bed on a flat plate or in an empty coconut shell. Arrange the fish on top and strew over the onion rings.

Crab and courgette ramekins with basil mayonnaise sauce

Serves 4

225g/8oz young courgettes, wiped
¹/₄ tsp salt
170g/6oz fresh white crab meat
few drops of lemon juice

For the dressing
15g/¹/₂oz basil leaves, chopped and pounded to a
purée, plus 4 whole leaves for decoration
2 tbsp mayonnaise
2 tbsp yoghurt
1–2 tsp hot water, if necessary

Grate the courgettes finely into a bowl. Mix with the salt and leave for 5–10 minutes. Gently squeeze out the excess moisture with your hands.

Mix very lightly with the crab meat, adding a few drops of lemon juice to taste. Take a quarter of the mixture and press into a small ramekin dish. Loosen the sides with a palette knife and invert on to a plate. Make 3 more moulds the same way. Mix the dressing ingredients to a smooth cream, adding a spot of hot water if too thick, and pour in a pool around each ramekin. Decorate with a tiny basil leaf and serve. (If you are using a whole crab, mix the brown meat with a little mustard, lemon juice and enough breadcrumbs to stiffen. Heap on to 4 large basil leaves and serve one with each ramekin on the same plate.)

LYNDA BROWN

Warm salmon and pink grapefruit salad

Serves 6

450g/1lb fresh salmon (boned and skinned weight)
salt and pepper
3 pink-fleshed grapefruit
prepared salad leaves, washed and dried
1–2 tbsp olive oil
45g/1½oz sliced hazelnuts
1–2 tbsp extra-virgin olive oil
1–2 tbsp balsamic vinegar

Cut the salmon into 2.5cm/1in cubes and season lightly. Using a sharp knife, cut all the peel and pith from the grapefruit, and cut the segments neatly from the central membrane. Arrange these segments on six plates, placing the salad leaves alongside. (This can be done in advance.)

Just before serving, heat the oil in a large frying pan and fry the fish over a moderate to high heat, turning frequently. Add the hazelnuts and continue to cook until the fish is opaque and the nuts lightly roasted. Spoon the hot fish and nuts down the centre of the prepared plate. Dribble over a little olive oil from a teaspoon, followed by a few drops of balsamic vinegar. Serve at once as a first course, handing round extra olive oil.

THANE PRINCE

Simone Sekers writes: BALSAMIC VINEGAR, like sun-dried tomatoes, has caught the imagination of the food world in recent times. A dark brown liquor made from grape must which may have been aged in wooden barrels for many years, it is far richer and more concentrated (and more expensive) than ordinary vinegar, and, like your best perfume, is used by the drop rather than the tablespoon. Mellow and sweet (a little caramelised sugar is added during its production) rather than thin and vinegary, it adds a sweet-sour dimension, and in fashionable circles is sometimes used sprinkled on strawberries and ripe pears as well as over fish and in dressings.

Home-preserved herrings

Now that we are being advised to eat fatty fish regularly, various kinds of salted or marinated herrings are ideal for healthy instant hors-d'oeuvres and first-course salads, and are one of the easiest things to prepare. A couple or so, kept in the refrigerator, are sufficient for 3–4 different salads.

To serve, slice thinly and arrange dainty amounts of various kinds of pre-served herrings as a herring smorgasbord, served with little dollops of beet-root or grated carrot and perhaps a horseradish dip. Alternatively, they can be chopped and mixed with a selection of the following ingredients to pro-duce a variety of appetising salads: apple/fennel/cucumber/gherkin/cel-ery/tomato/beetroot/cooked potato. Add fresh herbs/horseradish/spring onion, and bind with cream/crème fraiche/sour cream, plus a few drops of lemon or lime juice. Rollmops can be treated in the same way.

Salted herrings: These have a characteristic rich piquancy. Before using, taste and if necessary soak first in milk or milk and water to remove excess saltiness.

Remove the heads, clean and gut the fish (remove the tail, too, if you want). Soak overnight in vinegar. Drain well. For each pair of herrings, mix together 1 dsp of salt, 1 tsp sugar, 2–3 crushed allspice berries and 1 broken bay leaf. Sprinkle some of the mixture in a crock or glass dish and lay the first herring on top, belly side up. Sprinkle with a little more salt mixture, lay the second herring on top, finishing with the rest of the salt mixture. Cover with greaseproof paper, then put a weight on top. Turn regularly to ensure the herrings are in good contact with the brine. To use, chop into required lengths, and cut away the flesh from either side of backbone. They keep for 3–4 weeks.

Quick-salted herrings: Lay the cleaned herrings in a shallow bowl and cover with fine sea salt. Cover with cling film (or an upturned plate) and refrigerate overnight. Wash and use. They keep for 2 weeks in a covered plastic container, if extra salt and water to cover are added.

Salted herrings in olive oil: These are particularly delicious. Slice quick-salted fillets in two, chop into convenient lengths and store covered with olive oil in the refrigerator. Use as required with a little of the oil poured over.

Home-pickled herrings: For each pair of filleted herrings allow 1 dsp of sea salt, 1 scant dsp of sugar, 1 tsp brandy, and 1/4 tsp black/white/green peppercorns, pounded together in a mortar, plus 1 generous dsp of chopped dill. Spread some of the spice mixture on a dish. Sprinkle over some dill. Over this, lay the first fillet, skin side down. Repeat with the spice/dill mixture and lay the second fillet on top, flesh side down. Spread the remaining spice/dill mixture on top. Cover with greaseproof paper and put a weight on top. Leave for 24 hours. Serve carved into fine slivers, as you would gravadlax. They keep for 1 week.

LYNDA BROWN

See also: Marinated salmon with mint, p. 27.

Creamy fish pie

Always use more than one kind of fish for this pie, which can be adapted as you please. Thane Prince suggests you try a mixture of smoked and fresh haddock, or salmon with monkfish and a few prawns. Use the milk in which you poached the fish to make the sauce.

Serves 4–6

675g/1½lb mixed fish
approx. 420ml/14fl. oz milk
225g/8oz mushrooms, sliced
30g/1oz butter
juice of ½ lemon

For the sauce
30g/1oz butter
30g/1oz flour
milk reserved from poaching fish
120ml/4fl. oz single cream
1 tbsp chopped chives
1 tbsp grated lemon rind from a well-scrubbed lemon
salt and pepper

Topping
675g/1½lb potatoes, boiled and mashed
55g/2oz butter
4–6 anchovy fillets
2 tbsp grated cheese

Poach the fish in the milk for 4–5 minutes until opaque. Remove, reserving the milk, and flake the fish into a baking dish, removing all skin and bone. Fry the sliced mushrooms in the butter until most of the liquid from them has evaporated, add the lemon juice and cook 2–3 minutes more until the lemon juice evaporates, then spoon over the fish.

Make a white sauce in the usual way, adding the cream, chopped chives and lemon rind, plus salt and pepper to taste. Pour this over the fish. Beat the mashed potatoes with the butter and anchovy fillets, and use to cover the fish mixture. Sprinkle with the grated cheese and bake in a preheated oven, 180°C/350°F/gas mark 4, for 40–45 minutes.

THANE PRINCE

Fish pilaf

Fish pilafs are simple to make and are another tasty way of stretching fish. As with all pilafs, the spices and flavourings can be adapted as you see fit or according to what is to hand (the variation below is one example). The only thing to watch is not to overcook the fish.

Serves 3–4

450g/1lb firm white fish, skinned, boned and cut into
large chunks
1 onion, finely chopped
1 tbsp vegetable oil
1 tsp whole cumin seeds plus 1/2 tsp ground cumin
340g/12oz basmati rice
1–2 good pinches of powdered saffron or
1/2 tsp turmeric
360–420ml/12–14fl. oz water
1 bay leaf
pinch of salt

To finish
55g/2oz dried apricots, covered with boiling water and
left to plump up for 15–30 minutes
7–15g/1/4–1/2oz butter
2 tbsp each of raisins and pine nuts
55g/2oz prawns, defrosted and drained (optional)
1 tbsp finely chopped coriander or parsley

Soften the onions in the oil in a non-stick pan or heavy casserole. Stir in the cumin, fry for 1 minute, then add the rice and powdered saffron or turmeric (the latter is not a substitute and gives a different flavour, but colours the dish in approximately the same way). Stir until the rice is translucent, then distribute the fish over the top. Add the water, bay leaf and salt, using the poaching liquid from the apricots, plus extra to make up to the required amount. Bring to the boil, cover and cook over the gentlest heat possible until the liquid has evaporated, about 5–10 minutes.

Meanwhile, cut the apricots into slivers and fry them gently in the butter for 2–3 minutes in a small pan with the raisins and pine nuts until the raisins have plumped and the pine nuts are lightly browned. Once the water has been absorbed into the rice, stir this mixture gently into the pilaf, at the same time breaking up the fish into smaller pieces. Replace the lid, and leave the dish to stand with the heat turned off for 7–10 minutes, during which time the fish and rice will finish cooking. Mix in the prawns if using, scatter the herbs on top and serve immediately with a green or tomato salad.

Variation: In order to give the pilaf a more South-east Asian flavour, substitute 1–2 tsp of finely grated ginger and 1 finely chopped de-seeded green chilli for the cumin, saffron/turmeric and bay leaf, frying them for 1 minute once the onion has softened. Make up the required amount of liquid with the juice of 2 Seville oranges (or 1 sweet orange and 1 lemon when Seville oranges are not available). Cook the pilaf as described above. Just before serving, instead of the apricot/pine nut mixture, stir in 1 small chopped banana or cubes of fresh pineapple. Transfer to a serving platter, scatter with 30–55g/1–2 oz lightly toasted coconut flakes and surround with a garland of Yan-kit So's stir-fried mange-touts (*see* p. 158).

LYNDA BROWN

Simone Sekers writes: SAFFRON is the most expensive flavouring in the world: the distinctive red-orange strands are the stigmas of *Crocus sativus*, a small plant which can only be harvested by hand. The best way to buy it (and the best is supposed to come from La Mancha in Spain) is as whole strands. If it is the real thing, powdered saffron can be just as good, but very often it is not all it claims to be. If the powdered saffron you bought on holiday was a wonderful bargain, then it probably isn't saffron. I have also been 'had' by what looked like the real thing, but was actually the woollier, paler orange fibres of fake saffron, or safflower. Real saffron not only has the ability to colour paella, pilafs, risottos, fish soups and some English cakes a deep and appetising golden yellow, but also adds an inimitable flavour, at once spicy and almost medicinally bitter if used too generously (a fault not often encountered because of its price). As noted above, if you merely want to achieve colour, turmeric has the same effect, but if you want the authentic flavour as well, be prepared to spend about £1 for 0.25g of best 'Mancha quality' Spanish saffron, which is ample, however, to flavour a paella for about 10 people. It is widely available in delicatessens, Indian grocers, and from the spice racks of most supermarkets. To use the strands, infuse a pinch of them in a small amount of hot water and add both strands and liquid to the dish.

Smoked haddock soufflé with cumin

Serves 4

340g/12oz smoked haddock,
cooked in 300ml/10fl. oz milk
55g/2oz butter
1 small onion, finely chopped
1 heaped tbsp ground cumin
55g/2oz plain flour
4 egg yolks and 5 egg whites
a little Parmesan cheese (*see* p. 197)

Flake, skin and bone the fish. Melt the butter and fry the onion until golden. Add the cumin and fry, stirring, for 1–2 minutes. Stir in the flour and make a thick sauce in the usual way, using the strained milk from the fish. Cool a little, then stir in the egg yolks, one at a time, followed by the fish. Mix lightly but well. (The soufflé can be made up to this point and stored overnight in the refrigerator; warm carefully before continuing.)

Whisk the egg whites until stiff and fold gently into the fish mixture with a metal spoon. Pour into a well-buttered ovenproof dish sprinkled with the Parmesan. Cook in a preheated hot oven, 200°C/400°F/gas mark 6, for 30–35 minutes. The soufflé should be well risen and golden brown, but still a little runny in the centre. Serve as a supper dish or for brunch.

THANE PRINCE

Simone Sekers writes: SMOKED HADDOCK need no longer be simply haddock dyed yellow and flavoured with smoke substitute; more and more independent smokehouses offer their own versions of the real thing: mild, delicate, sweet and juicy. For a real treat, use Finnan 'haddie' for this recipe, which is smoked on the bone. It will be more fiddly to deal with, but the reward will be in the flavour.

Mussels in piquant tomato sauce

Serves 4

1½kg/3lb cleaned and prepared mussels (*see* p. 60)
¼ bottle dry white wine
1 medium onion, chopped
2–3 parsley stalks
4–5 black peppercorns

For the sauce
2 shallots, finely chopped
2 sticks celery, chopped
2 tbsp olive oil
2 plump cloves garlic, finely chopped
400g/14oz tinned tomatoes, chopped
200ml/⅓pt mussel liquor
1 small dry red chilli, de-seeded and crumbled
1 tsp grated lemon zest
salt and pepper
2 tbsp chopped fresh coriander
2 tbsp chopped fresh parsley

Bring the wine to the boil and add the onion, parsley stalks and pepper-corns. Simmer for 60 seconds, add the mussels, turn the heat up high and cook them for 2–3 minutes, stirring well, by which time they should have opened wide. Remove the mussels from the pan with a slotted spoon and allow to cool, discarding any which remain closed. Remove the mussels from their shells and store, covered, in the refrigerator, until needed. Strain the mussel liquor through a double layer of muslin and boil until reduced to 210ml/7fl. oz.

To make the sauce, fry the shallots and celery in the oil until transparent. Add the garlic and fry for a further 60 seconds. Put in all the remaining ingredients except the fresh herbs and simmer for 10–15 minutes. Stir in the mussels, coriander and parsley and correct the seasoning. Serve with fresh pasta, rice or topped with puff pastry as a pie, cooked for 15–20 minutes in a very hot oven, 220°C/425°F/gas mark 7, until the pastry is golden brown.

THANE PRINCE

Grilled herrings with mint and lime stuffing

Serves 4

4 large, filleted herrings

For the stuffing
4–5 tbsp chopped mint
1 tbsp chopped raisins
1/2–1 tsp lightly toasted and crushed cumin seeds
finely grated rind of 1 well-scrubbed lime

Mix together the stuffing ingredients and spread over the inside of each fillet. Fold over and secure the belly flap with a cocktail stick. Make two diagonal cuts along both sides of the backbone, place in a dish and grill, turning once, until cooked, about 5–7 minutes. Serve with wedges of lime, a green salad and rice or potatoes.

LYNDA BROWN

Fish steaks baked in lemon cream

Serves 4

4 thick fish steaks such as cod, hake or halibut
120ml/4fl. oz thick plain, preferably Greek-style,
yoghurt
120ml/4fl. oz single cream
1 tbsp finely grated onion
finely grated scrubbed rind and juice of 1 lemon, plus
very thin slices of lemon

Wipe the fish steaks and lay them side by side in a buttered ovenproof dish. Drain the yoghurt until it is almost solid by tipping it into a sieve lined with muslin over a bowl. Mix with the other ingredients to form a thick topping (you may not need all the lemon juice), and spoon over the surface of the fish. Leave for at least 2 hours in the refrigerator, covered. Bake at 180°C/350°F/gas mark 4 for 25–30 minutes. The topping will set to a creamy curd and there will be a little clear juice surrounding the fish. Decorate with lemon slices and serve with saffron-flavoured rice and a crisp green salad.

LYNDA BROWN

Hake with fennel and apple purée

Serves 4

7–15g/¼–½oz butter for frying
4 large hake steaks
4 tbsp vermouth

For the sauce
340g/12oz chopped bulb fennel
1 large sweet eating apple, peeled, cored and sliced
(approx. 170g/6oz prepared weight)
2–3 strips scrubbed lemon peel
up to 15g/½oz butter

Start with the sauce. Gently cook the fennel and apple with the lemon peel in a little water in a covered pan for 20–25 minutes until soft. Discard the peel and blend to a smooth purée. Return to the pan through a sieve, pressing hard through the sieve to extract as much of the purée as possible. Continue to cook until the mixture is reduced by about a third, or until thick without any trace of wateriness. Beat in butter to taste and reserve. (This can be done in advance.)

Seal the fish steaks on both sides over a high heat in a knob of butter in a non-stick frying pan. Turn the heat right down, pour over 3 tbsp of vermouth, cover and cook gently until the fish is just cooked, about 5–7 minutes depending on the thickness of the fish. Turn off the heat and let the fish relax for 3–4 minutes, then transfer to hot plates. Boil down any juices until syrupy, add the rest of the vermouth and dribble over the fish. Surround with the hot apple and fennel purée and serve with rice.

LYNDA BROWN

Baked salt cod and potatoes

Once a curiosity here, salt cod is becoming increasingly popular. Currently a fashionable dish in London restaurants, the general reaction seems to be that you either love it or hate it. If you have never tried salt cod before, this colourful Portuguese fish and potato pie from Thane Prince, where the salt cod marries with a rich tomato sauce, is a good dish to start with. The fish needs to be soaked first to remove the excess salt, and it has a gluey, sticky texture which means it does not flake as easily as other fish. For this recipe you may need to use a knife to scrape off any flesh which remains on the skin. All the preparation can be done in advance and the pie assembled when you come to bake it.

Serves 4

450g/1lb dried salt cod
900g/2lb waxy potatoes
1 large onion, chopped
3–4 cloves garlic, crushed
2 tbsp olive oil
2 tinned pimentoes, sliced
400g/14oz tinned tomatoes (or, for a smoother sauce,
use tomato passata)
55g/2oz black olives, stoned and sliced (*see* p. 117)
1 tsp capers, chopped
1/2 tsp dried mixed herbs
pepper
300ml/10fl. oz water
1 dsp tomato purée

Soak the cod in plenty of cold water for 48 hours, changing the water 4 times. Place in a saucepan with sufficient fresh water to cover, bring to the boil, remove from the heat and allow to cool. Remove the skin and bone and tear the flesh into small pieces. Parboil the potatoes in their skins for 15 minutes, cool, peel, and cut into thin slices.

For the sauce, fry the onion and garlic slowly in the olive oil until transparent and beginning to turn brown. Add the pimentoes, tomatoes, olives, capers, herbs and pepper (the fish and olives should contribute sufficient salt), followed by the water with the tomato purée stirred in. Mix well and simmer for 5 minutes. Stir the fish into the sauce.

To assemble the pie, oil an earthenware casserole dish, put a layer of potatoes on the bottom, saving the best slices for the top. Pour the fish mixture over and top with the remaining potatoes. Brush with a little olive oil, cover and bake in a preheated oven, 160°C/325°F/gas mark 3, for 1 1/2–2 hours, removing the lid 30 minutes before the end of cooking to brown the potatoes.

THANE PRINCE

Editor's note: I must confess to liking peas with this dish. If you prefer, 1 tbsp fresh parsley (or a mixture of parsley and coriander) can be used instead of the dried mixed herbs. If you cannot find tinned pimentoes use 1 large red pepper, roasted under the grill or in the oven and then peeled.

Simone Sekers writes: SALT COD or salt fish as it is sometimes called since it can be cod, large haddock or hake, is dried after it has been liberally salted, so it is both hard and very salty. Although a product of Norway, its most appreciative market is in Mediterranean countries, where the powerful preservation methods are appropriate. Look for it in Spanish, Italian and even Greek food shops. Try to pick a piece from the thick end of the fillet, rather than the tail end. The harder and yellower the fish, the longer it will need to be soaked, in several changes of water. Recently, however, I have found a more lightly salted cod that only needs an overnight soak – it looks whiter and softer than the driftwood texture of classic salt cod, but has a less distinctive flavour.

Moroccan grilled fish with chermoula

This recipe, one of Claudia Roden's, comes from a woman in the old Jewish quarter of Marrakesh. She explains that the marinade is too strong-tasting to use with delicate fish but works very well for cod, haddock and whiting.

Serves 4

4 thick cod steaks

For the marinade
1 small onion
2 cloves garlic
120ml/4fl. oz olive oil or light vegetable oil
juice of 1 lemon
1 tbsp paprika
1 tbsp cumin
good bunch of coriander leaves
good pinch of cayenne pepper
salt

Mix the marinade ingredients and pour over the fish. Leave the fish steaks in the marinade for about 1 hour. Put them under a medium grill for 5–6 minutes, turning them over once. The fish is cooked when the flesh begins to flake away from the bone as you cut it with the point of a knife.

CLAUDIA RODEN

Grilled fish steaks with tamarind sauce

This is another simple but exotic recipe from Claudia Roden. The sweet and sour flavour of the sauce, she writes, makes a change from herbs and lemon, and is good with all kinds of fish.

Serves 2

2 fish steaks – cod, haddock, salmon
1¹/₂ tbsp olive oil
salt and pepper

For the sauce
1 clove garlic, crushed
1 tbsp olive oil
1 tbsp tamarind paste
120ml/4fl. oz water
1 tsp sugar or to taste
2cm/³/₄ in piece of fresh ginger, grated or crushed

For the sauce, fry the garlic in the olive oil till the aroma rises, then stir in the tamarind paste. Add the water, sugar and ginger (I crush it in a garlic press to extract the juice), stir well and simmer for about 10 minutes, adding water if necessary.

Turn the fish in the olive oil and sprinkle with salt and pepper. Put it under the grill on a fireproof dish and let it cook for about 8 minutes, or until the flesh just begins to flake when you pierce it with the point of a knife, turning it over once. Serve at once, with the sauce.

CLAUDIA RODEN

Simone Sekers writes: TAMARIND is used as a sharp, acid flavouring in Indian and some Middle Eastern dishes. The dried pulp of the fruit is sold in dark brown blocks resembling toffee in Indian grocers and good delicatessens; the block should not be rock hard but should bend a little, or the necessary reconstitution in water will take a long time. Lemon juice can sometimes be used instead, but will not give the distinctive tamarind taste (or colour). A ready-made tamarind paste is also available which has a good flavour and is easy to use.

Editor's note: To make tamarind paste from dried tamarind, break off a small lump, cover with hot water and leave for 10 minutes to soften and swell. Push hard through a sieve to extract as much pulp as possible, and use as directed.

As a substitute for tamarind, the South East Asian culinary expert Jennifer Brennan suggests using 1 tbsp molasses to 3 tbsp lime juice, stirring the lime juice into the molasses until well mixed.

TUNA, SWORDFISH AND SHARK

The next three recipes appeared together in an article by Thane Prince, who had the following advice to offer:

'These fish have much in common in their preparation and cooking. Their firm, meaty flesh and few bones mean that they can be enjoyed by all the family. They can be cubed for kebabs, grilled and baked, all with great success, and can hold their own in robust fish casseroles. Marinating in a mixture of olive oil and lemon juice for an hour enhances their flavour. For an oriental taste, use a little soy sauce and grated fresh ginger root in your marinade.

'One of the commonest mistakes when grilling fish is to overcook it. A tuna steak will cook and dry out under a hot grill much more quickly than a pork chop. Once grilled to perfection, top the fish with a spoonful of your favourite sauce, for example aïoli (*see* p. 136).'

Tuna with sun-dried tomatoes

Serves 4

4 tuna steaks
3 tbsp olive oil
juice of 1 lemon
1–2 cloves garlic, or to taste, chopped
6 sun-dried tomatoes (*see* p. 30)
4 tsp chives
salt and pepper

Marinate the fish in the oil, lemon juice and garlic for 1 hour. Prepare 4 squares of foil and spoon a little marinade on to each one. Place a piece of fish in the middle of each square and spoon over the rest of the marinade sharing it equally between them. Snip the sun-dried tomatoes with scissors and divide between the steaks. Sprinkle over the chives, season with salt and pepper, gather up each piece of foil into a parcel, sealing the edges well, and place on a baking sheet. Bake in a preheated oven, 180°C/350°F/gas mark 4, for 15–20 minutes. Serve with the cooking juices poured over, and rice and salad to accompany.

THANE PRINCE

Baked swordfish with leeks (or mushrooms)

Serves 4

4 swordfish steaks
salt and pepper
30g/1oz butter
2 tbsp olive oil
2–3 medium leeks, cleaned and finely sliced
180ml/6fl. oz dry white wine
150ml/5fl. oz double cream

Wipe the swordfish, season lightly and set aside. Melt the butter and oil in a cast-iron gratin dish and gently fry the leeks until softened. Arrange the fish on the leeks and pour over the wine. Cover the dish with foil and bake in the centre of a preheated oven, 180°C/350°F/gas mark 4, for 20–25 minutes or until the fish is opaque throughout.

Remove the fish to a warmed serving dish and keep warm. Place the gratin dish on the hob. Reduce the cooking juices by one third by rapid boiling, and then stir in the cream. Heat to boiling point, taste and correct the seasoning. Spoon the sauce over the fish and serve with plain boiled rice.

Variation: Instead of leeks, 225g/8oz finely sliced mushrooms can be used.

THANE PRINCE

Shark and chick pea casserole

Serves 6

675–900g/1½–2lb shark, skinned, boned and cubed
flour for dusting
salt and pepper
1 medium onion, chopped
1–2 cloves garlic, finely chopped
2 tbsp olive oil
6 medium tomatoes, skinned and chopped
90ml/3fl. oz white wine or water with a squeeze of
lemon juice
340g/12oz tinned chick peas, drained
1 tbsp tomato purée
1–2 dried chilli peppers
340g/12oz courgettes, sliced

Lightly dust the cubes of shark with seasoned flour. In a deep casserole dish, fry the onion and garlic in the oil until softened. Add the fish and fry for 2–3 minutes, turning until it is sealed on all sides (you may need to add a little more oil to the pan). Remove from the pan and reserve. Add the chopped tomatoes to the casserole and stir until they begin to soften and cook. Add the wine or water, chick peas, tomato purée, chilli, salt and pepper. Stir well and simmer gently for about 5 minutes. Return the shark to the pan and add the courgettes. Stir everything together and cook for a further 5–10 minutes until the fish and courgettes are cooked but not soft. Serve immediately with rice or couscous.

Simone Sekers writes: TUNA, SWORDFISH AND SHARK are being found at adventurous fish counters around the country, north and south. Tuna looks not unlike steak – dark red and very meaty – while swordfish and shark are paler. All three are expensive, but there isn't much waste, there are few irritating bones and, as all are densely fleshed fish, it is possible to get away with only about 110g/4oz per person. It is a good idea to check with the fishmonger whether the swordfish is fresh or frozen – I have had some very dreary frozen fish on occasion. It is always fresh at Marks & Spencer. As tuna has the strongest flavour, it can be partnered with other strong flavours (and could be substituted for shark in the recipe above). Shark and swordfish are more delicate. All can be very good cooked on a barbecue when fresh but, being dry, will need lubrication in the form of a marinade or oil.

See also: Poached salmon, p. 125; Salmon with elderflowers, p. 105; Salmon with orange mousseline, watercress and orange sauce, p. 227; Salmon with ginger sauce, p. 134; Barbecued scallops with Pernod sauce, p. 133.

On the Wild Side

IN THIS CHAPTER I have drawn together recipes for game, mushrooms, and some of our most common hedgerow fruits. I have also included a couple of recipes for nettles, probably the most accessible wild food of all, and a traditional springtime herb. Collectively they represent a taste of the wild, a taste which has been revived in recent times and one which seems to be increasing in appeal daily.

The reasons for this revival are twofold. The far greater availability of game in supermarkets and in the High Street, coupled with the proliferation of farmed game, particularly venison and pheasant, has meant that game is accessible to everyone, and at affordable prices (a pheasant these days costs no more than chicken, and venison is around the same price as beef). High in visual appeal and flavour, each type of game has its own distinctive taste, which may be milder or stronger depending on the age, length of hanging, habitat and so on. Being lean and low in saturated fats, game offers a more healthy alternative to traditional red meats, another reason for its rise in popularity; and it now features regularly on restaurant menus, which has helped to give us all the confidence to try game dishes at home.

Aided by our fascination with French, Italian and foreign food in general, the popularity of wild mushrooms has grown in a similar way. Alongside these influences, increasing concern about modern methods of production has prompted an interest in naturally grown foods of every kind, including food which grows wild and is free for the picking. Such foods – berries from the hedgerows, mushrooms from the woods, wild thyme among the heather, watercress from the streams – are natural partners to game, and, indeed, form part of their diet. The two complement each other in a way that takes us back to our traditional and time-honoured way of eating food in season. Beginning with advice on game from Simone Sekers, this chapter is thus a celebration of country flavours, there to be enjoyed for their own sake, whether bought, or as part of nature's free (and therefore all the more pleasurable) bounty.

GAME

The season for feathered game opens on 12 August (grouse) and continues until the end of January, although pigeons have no close season. Furred game, such as rabbit, hare and venison, also has no close season, although hare should not be sold from March to July. The supply of venison depends on the breed.

Hanging game: There is less stomach, these days, for game hung so long that the tail feathers drop out of their own accord. Most game should be hung, however, unplucked and undrawn, for a minimum of 5 days in order to develop its flavour and tenderness. It is essential that it is kept where there is a freely circulating current of cold, dry air. If the weather is damp and warm, 5 days is the maximum time for hanging.

The best guide to the age of hares and rabbits is to examine their claws; if they are well covered with fur the animal is less than a year old and will make good tender eating. Use hares of this age for roasting or braising. Older, well-exercised hares need long, slow cooking, but will have a wonderfully rich flavour.

Venison: Farmed venison is now generally available and is in many ways preferable to the wild version. It will be reliably tender, and its flavour more universally acceptable to those who prefer their game without a too-pronounced gamey flavour. If using wild venison with no idea of its age, your motto should be: don't hesitate, marinate. A basic mixture of red wine and olive oil, in the proportions of 3:1, with a sliced onion and carrot, peppercorns and a bay leaf or two, should be poured over the meat at least 12 hours before cooking. Farmed venison rarely needs such treatment.

Game accompaniments: Most game, being dry meat, needs some lubrication apart from its accompanying sauce or gravy. Although redcurrant jelly is the most familiar accompaniment, rowan jelly (*see* p. 108) is even better. It has a unique tart, smoky flavour which complements most game – after all, certain wild game may well have fed on rowan berries. One firm I have found, Cottage Delights, sells a particularly good rowan jelly. Look for it in farm shops and delicatessens. Baxter's also make it. Failing that, try a combination of black cherry jam, cinnamon and port (warm half a jar of jam gently with a generous glass of port and a 2.5cm/1in stick of cinnamon), sharpened with the juice of a Seville orange if you have it, a dessertspoon of lemon juice if you don't.

SIMONE SEKERS

Game stock and game soups

The carcass and leftovers of game should never be wasted but turned into a flavoursome stock. This can be kept in the freezer and used either as a base for future sauces and soups, beaten into vegetable purées or for cooking dried pulses such as the small green or brown lentils which go so well with game, and which acquire a lovely flavour when cooked with game stock and a stick of cinnamon or the Chinese spice, star anise.

Make the stock in the usual way, browning the bones or carcass first, adding a selection of chopped vegetables such as onions, carrots, celery, leeks, a little swede or parsnip and perhaps a tomato, bacon rinds if you have them, and peppercorns, thyme and parsley. Try to include a piece of pork rind (or even better, a split pork trotter), as this helps to enrich the stock. A glass of wine or a splash of sherry can be added if desired. Cover with water and simmer very gently for 2–3 hours, taking off any scum as it rises. Strain, and then simmer down further to concentrate the flavour.

If the stock is of good heart, with a rich clean flavour, it can be used as it is as a delicious game consommé. For this, you will probably need to clarify it further with an egg white: whisk the egg white lightly, then stir it into the stock set over a low flame. Let it come gently to the boil and barely simmer for a few minutes. The egg white will form a crust, collecting all the impurities from the stock. Strain very carefully through a sieve lined with muslin. The strained stock will be crystal clear, and is best served in the traditional way, with small rounds of beef marrow scooped from a marrow bone, cut into thin slices and added to the soup at the last moment (they will float on top). Alternatively, you can add a few shreds of carrot, celery and leek, or perhaps spring onion, to the hot broth, simmer for 1–2 minutes and then serve; or serve the consommé plain, garnished with a few croutons, fried in butter, or a sprinkling of chopped chives, tarragon or chervil.

If the stock is thin, use it as a base for other soups, such as the chestnut soup on p. 223, or a simple lentil and vegetable soup with lentils, onions or leeks, diced turnip and parsnip.

LYNDA BROWN

Game and pork terrine

Game terrines are a popular way of using up the less tender meat, or game which has been badly shot, saving the choice breast fillets for another meal. This is a simple recipe for pheasant, from Simone Sekers, which can be adapted to suit whatever game you may have in whatever quantity.

Use a mixture of three-quarters finely chopped belly pork to one-quarter chopped pheasant meat, or half and half if you prefer. Season the meat with salt, pepper and a pinch of ground allspice, and add a good glass of Madeira or medium-dry sherry. Cook in an ovenproof dish lined with bacon rashers for about 1½ hours at 160°C/325°F/gas mark 3, standing the dish in a roasting tin of hot water, replenishing the water as necessary. The terrine is done when the meat has shrunk from the sides of the dish. Cool, and store in the refrigerator for 1–2 days before eating. Serve with a mild jelly, such as redcurrant, or with pickled damsons or walnuts and eat within a week. (In the old days, when fat wasn't such a dirty word and pork had more fat on it, enough fat emerged in the cooking to seal the terrine and thus keep it for at least a fortnight. Now, less fat equals less keeping quality.)

The breast fillets, meanwhile, can be cooked swiftly under a hot grill, brushed first with olive oil, and served on a bed of any of the following: braised red cabbage; peeled and sliced Cox's apples sautéed in butter and finished with a mixture of orange juice and Calvados; raw beetroot, grated and stir-fried until very hot but still crunchy. Make sure the meat remains pink – overcooked it becomes tough and you will wish you had made the bird into a casserole instead.

Note: While any game can be used for this terrine, if using hare there should be a slightly higher proportion of pork as hare has a stronger flavour than most other game.

SIMONE SEKERS

Potted pheasant

Any strongish flavoured meat or game, writes Thane Prince, such as grouse, beef or tongue, can be potted this way. 'It is ideal for using up smaller quantities of meat, or perhaps just the legs if the breasts are used for another dish. Allow about 55g/2oz butter per 225g/8oz cooked meat.'

Serves 6–8

1 pheasant, roasted
approx. 170g/6oz butter
freshly grated nutmeg
salt
cayenne pepper

Cut the meat from the carcass, taking care to remove any splintered bone and lead shot. Put the meat in a food processor with 110g/4oz of the butter and process until you have a fine paste. Season to taste with nutmeg, salt and cayenne pepper. Pack the meat into a suitable pot and level the surface. Heat the remaining butter gently and pour it over the paste, leaving the milky sediment behind; it should cover the paste completely and form an airtight seal. Store in the refrigerator for at least 24 hours to allow the flavours to develop. Serve with hot buttered toast.

THANE PRINCE

Roast grouse with white currants

Grouse is best when roasted pink. For this, you need young tender birds; as Thane Prince said in her article, you will have to judge whether the bird you have is big enough for one or two servings.

Serves 1–2

1 plump young grouse, cleaned
55g/2oz white currants
45g/1½oz butter
salt and pepper
1 tbsp olive oil
flour for dredging
60ml/2fl. oz dry sherry
150ml/5fl. oz meat or game stock

Mash the white currants with the butter, reserving a few for garnish. Stuff the bird with this and season well. Place the bird in a roasting dish, pour over the olive oil and dredge with flour. Roast in a hot oven, 220°C/425°F/gas mark 7, for 10 minutes, then turn the heat down and roast at 180°C/350°F/gas mark 4 for a further 10–15 minutes, according to taste, basting the bird with the pan juices from time to time.

Remove the grouse and allow to stand in a warm oven while you make the gravy. Pour off most of the fat and deglaze the pan with sherry. Pour in the stock and bring to the boil, stirring and scraping the meat juices. When the sauce is reduced by one third place the grouse on a serving dish, glaze the bird lightly with a little of the sauce, and decorate with the remaining currants. Serve the remainder of the sauce separately.

THANE PRINCE

Betty Allen's breast of pheasant with a whisky and grape sauce

This recipe comes from Betty Allen of Airds Hotel in Port Apin, Scotland; her cooking, which now has a Michelin star, is among the best you will find. It is a good dinner-party dish – quick to do yet elegant. Another of her recipes, for Atholl Brose, can be found on p. 238.

Serves 4–6

4 tender boned pheasant breasts, skin removed

For the sauce
2 shallots or 1/2 small onion, finely chopped
approx. 30g/1oz unsalted butter for frying
150ml/5fl. oz red wine
150ml/5fl. oz good chicken stock
2–3 tbsp whisky
150ml/5fl. oz double cream
110g/4oz black grapes, halved and de-seeded
salt and pepper

Start with the sauce, which can be half-cooked in advance. Soften the shallots in a little of the butter in a medium-sized non-stick frying pan. Add the wine, stock and whisky and boil down to 2–3 tbsp. If leaving, cover at this stage.

Heat the rest of the butter in a large non-stick pan and brown the breasts on both sides. Turn down the heat and continue to cook, for approximately 5–7 minutes each side. Remove the pheasant and keep warm. Add any cooking juices and the cream to the sauce. Boil up, add the grapes, check for seasoning and cook for a further 2 minutes.

Slice each breast into three and arrange on hot plates. Pour the sauce around. Serve with a smooth potato and celeriac purée, and spinach or shredded cabbage stir-fried with some finely chopped walnuts.

Variation: Using essentially the same recipe, you can produce the following richly flavoured braise for pheasant or grouse legs.

Cut the legs through the knee joint. Brown all over in butter, add the shallots, soften, then follow with the wine, whisky and stock, plus a sprig of thyme and 3–4 crushed juniper berries. Cover, leaving the lid very slightly ajar, and simmer over the lowest heat possible for 50–60 minutes, turning the pieces from time to time. Remove the legs and pop under the grill for 4–5 minutes to crisp the skin.

Meanwhile, strain the sauce, pressing the debris hard against the sieve with the back of a spoon. Add grapes as before, plus cream to taste (this can be left out if preferred). Thicken slightly if you wish (I use potato flour – *see* p. 39 – but you could also use *beurre manié*), and pour around the legs. Serve with brown rice.

LYNDA BROWN

Pheasant in red wine (Fagiano in salmi)

This is a glorious, rich-tasting dish.

Serves 6

3 young tender hen pheasants
55g/2oz butter plus 2 tbsp oil for frying
2 slices unsmoked bacon, chopped
1 large onion, chopped
1 large carrot, chopped
2 cloves garlic, finely chopped
2 anchovies, finely chopped
1 stick celery and leaves, chopped
150ml/5fl. oz Marsala
1 bottle red wine
1 sprig sage
2 sprigs rosemary
3 bay leaves
5 cloves
1 tsp cinnamon
12 juniper berries
salt and pepper

Sauté the pheasants in a mixture of the butter and oil in a large casserole, turning them to brown them all over, then take them out. Drain off some of the fat, leaving enough to fry the bacon and onion. When the onion is soft, add the carrot and garlic, and when the aroma rises, add the anchovies and celery. Pour in the Marsala and the wine and add the sage, rosemary, bay leaves, cloves, cinnamon, juniper berries, salt and pepper. Put the pheasants back in the casserole, add enough water just to cover the birds, and simmer, covered, for 30–45 minutes until tender, turning the birds over at least once. Ladle most of the sauce into another pan and boil down to a rich consistency. Carve the birds at the table, handing round the sauce separately.

If you prefer, you can also cook the pheasants, covered, in a hot oven, 200°C/400°F/gas mark 6, for 45–60 minutes. CLAUDIA RODEN

Roast partridge with blackberry sauce

Partridge is at its best in mid to late autumn, writes Simone Sekers, and makes an unusual and delicious special-occasion dinner: 'Wild elder-berries work well with this recipe, but frozen bilberries or blackberries are a good alternative. Grouse may also be cooked in the same way.'

Serves 2

2 plump partridges

For the sauce
30g/1oz butter
2 sprigs of lemon thyme, or ordinary thyme with a
small piece of scrubbed lemon rind
salt and pepper
4 rashers unsmoked streaky bacon
2 shallots or 1 red onion, peeled and finely chopped
150ml/5fl. oz giblet or chicken stock
4 tbsp red wine
4 tbsp blackberries (or elderberries or bilberries)

Preheat the oven to 200°C/400°F/gas mark 6. Work the butter with the herbs and a little salt and pepper, and put some into the cavity of each bird. Stretch the bacon rashers with a knife and wrap them around the partridges. Roast in a small baking dish for about 30 minutes, starting them on their sides and turning them over after 10 minutes. Lower the oven temperature to 180°C/350°F/gas mark 4 at this point, and put them breast side up for the final 10 minutes.

While they are cooking, simmer the shallots or onion, stock and wine until the onion is soft and the liquid reduced by about a third. Remove the partridges to a warm plate and leave them to rest in the switched-off oven. Pour off the fat from the roasting dish, add the shallot and wine mixture and bring to the boil, scraping up any residue from the pan. Add the berries and cook until they have softened and the flavours are well blended, about 10 minutes. The flavour should be mellow rather than sweet. If it is a little too sharp, add half a teaspoon of redcurrant jelly. Serve with a gratin of potatoes and some briefly cooked Brussels sprouts, chopped roughly and mixed with a few chopped celery leaves and a good knob of unsalted butter.

SIMONE SEKERS

Oven-grilled mallard

Mallard, or wild duck, writes Simone Sekers, has all the flavour of domestic duck, with a good deal less fat: 'It is excellent for those who do not like the "gamey" flavour of game. One bird is ample for two, which makes it good value. It is also very good cold.'

Serves 4

2 mallard
4 tbsp groundnut oil
2 wine glasses (approx. 240–300ml/8–10fl. oz) port
10 allspice berries, crushed
freshly ground black pepper
4 rashers unsmoked streaky bacon
150–240ml/5–8fl. oz water

Split the mallard down the middle, using a heavy knife. Trim away and reserve the wing tips and backbones, and put the halves in a shallow dish. Mix the oil, port, allspice and pepper together and pour over the ducks. Leave them for about 4 hours, turning frequently.

Preheat the oven to 220°C/425°F/gas mark 7. Arrange a greased cake rack over a roasting tin, put the mallard halves on top, cut side down, and place a bacon rasher over each of them. Cook for about 25 minutes, basting them with the pan juices or, if these are meagre, some of the marinade.

Meanwhile, strain the rest of the marinade into a pan, add the trimmings from the ducks and a little extra water and simmer while the birds are cooking. Remove the birds to a serving dish, add the stock to the pan juices and boil together until the flavours are well blended to make a light gravy. Arrange on a bed of braised red cabbage and apple (*see* p. 224) which can be cooked the day before and reheated.

Note: There is a risk of wild duck tasting fishy (though not the mallard you find oven-ready in supermarkets). Give those you buy from a game dealer a good sniff – your nose should tell you. Instead of the port/allspice combination, marinate any suspect birds in a mixture of gin and olive oil (say 2 tbsp gin and 4 tbsp olive oil) for at least 2 hours, using this mixture to baste the birds while they are roasting. This counteracts the fish flavour, adds that of juniper berries (from the gin), breaks down any potential toughness, and lubricates the flesh at the same time. Alternatively, put an onion in the cavity [or an orange – Ed.] when cooking the bird.

SIMONE SEKERS

Venison and pear bigarade

Serves 4

675g/1¹/₂lb stewing venison, cut into 2.5cm/1in cubes
7g/¹/₄oz butter and 1–2 tbsp olive oil for frying
150ml/5fl. oz red wine plus 1 dsp wine vinegar
1.25cm/¹/₂in stick cinnamon, plus 6 coriander seeds (or
¹/₂ tsp each of the ground spice)
3–4 allspice berries
good grating of fresh nutmeg
2 tbsp Seville marmalade (not too much peel) dissolved
in a little hot water
110g/4oz dried pears, sliced down the middle
into halves

To finish
juice of ¹/₂–1 Seville orange, plus rind
1 tsp potato flour (*see* p. 39) slaked in 1 tbsp water

Brown the meat in a heavy casserole dish in the butter and olive oil. Pour in the wine and wine vinegar, let it bubble for a couple of minutes, then add the spices and marmalade dissolved in hot water.

Add just enough water to cover the meat, and bring to the boil. Cover very tightly (insert a sheet of greaseproof paper between dish and lid) and transfer to a low oven, 140°C/275°F/gas mark 1. Cook for 2–2¹/₂ hours until the meat is tender, adding extra water if the sauce seems to be drying up too soon. An hour before the end, lay the pears on top of the meat where they should soften without becoming too mushy.

Remove the meat and pears to a serving dish, arranging the pears around the outside and heaping the meat in the middle. Check the sauce, adding Seville orange juice to taste. Thicken with the potato flour liquid, adding it gradually, a teaspoon at a time. Bring back to the boil, pour over the meat, garnish with a wisp of orange rind and serve. Rice and spinach are good accompaniments.

LYNDA BROWN

Simone Sekers writes: SEVILLE ORANGES, also called bitter oranges if they come from other parts of Spain, have a tantalisingly short season – 6 weeks from the middle of January. Although also called 'marmalade' oranges because that is their major use in this country, their sharp juice is particularly good in game dishes – see also the following recipe for Cumbrian hare – and *canard à l'orange* really can be restored to glory if the sauce is made with Seville rather than sweet orange juice. Use it, too, in fish dishes instead of lemon juice, and include it in the stuffing for rich meats such as goose, pork and shoulder of lamb. The oranges can be frozen very successfully to prolong their season. When squeezing the juice from the fresh fruit, pour some hot water over them first so that they release their juice more easily.

Cumbrian hare with rowan jelly

This is a marvellous, powerful, sweet-tasting dish, again from Simone Sekers, with an almost chocolate richness which brings out the best of hare's strong gamey flavour.

Serves 4

front and back legs of 1 hare, jointed (keep the saddle
for another dish – *see* following recipe)
a little dripping, lard or oil for frying
3 small onions, each stuck with a clove
1 sprig dried thyme
450g/1lb jar of rowan jelly; or redcurrant jelly plus the
juice of 1 lemon (*see* note below)
1 wine glass (approx. 150ml/5fl. oz) port
salt and freshly ground pepper
1–2 tsp potato flour (optional) (*see* p. 39)

Season the hare joints and brown them briefly in a little dripping, lard or oil. Pack them into a stoneware casserole. Brown the whole onions and add them to the hare. Bury the thyme among the meat and onions and empty the pot of jelly all over. Add the port, some salt, and plenty of pepper.

Cover with a lid of foil and the casserole lid, stand the casserole in a baking tin of hot water and cook slowly in the oven, at 150°C/300°F/gas mark 2 for about 2 hours for a young hare, or 140°C/275°F/gas mark 1 for anything up to 5 hours for an old one. The juices can be thickened with 1–2 tsp of potato flour slaked in a little water if you wish. A good alternative to lemon juice is the juice of a Seville orange when available.

Note: Redcurrant jelly produces a much sweeter dish than rowan jelly (*see* p. 108), even with the lemon or orange juice. If you prefer, use a 340g/12oz jar of redcurrant jelly, making up the rest with water.

SIMONE SEKERS

Saddle of hare with grapefruit and thyme

Serves 4

1 saddle of hare on the bone
1½ small juicy grapefruit
1 tbsp olive oil
6 allspice berries, lightly crushed
6–8 sprigs fresh thyme

To finish
150ml/5fl. oz red wine
2–3 tsp redcurrant/quince/bramble jelly

Remove the silvery membrane from the back of the saddle with a sharp knife, cutting as close to the membrane as possible. Lay the saddle in an ovenproof dish (an oval gratin dish is ideal) into which the hare will just fit comfortably. Mix the juice of half a grapefruit with the oil, add the allspice and pour over the hare, scattering the thyme beneath and above. Marinate for 2–4 hours, turning the hare frequently.

Preheat the oven to 220°C/425°F/gas mark 7. Roast the hare for about 15–20 minutes. Do not overcook: the meat is done when a few beads of red juice are showing on the surface. Remove and let it rest for 10 minutes in a warm place.

Meanwhile, halve the remaining grapefruit and cut out the segments. They should be free from skin and pith. To make the sauce, deglaze the pan juices with the wine, scraping up all the residue. Stir in the jelly to taste and cook for 3–4 minutes until the flavours have blended, adding a little extra grapefruit juice if liked, and a few tablespoons of stock or water if the sauce is reducing down too much. At the last moment toss in the grapefruit segments to heat through. Carve the hare into long thin fillets (don't forget the nugget of underfillet). Spoon over the glaze, and serve immediately on hot plates. A simple parsnip purée, scattered with a few pine nuts fried in butter, and some pasta make excellent accompaniments.

LYNDA BROWN

Rabbit stew with button onions (Kouneli stifatho)

This Greek dish, writes Claudia Roden, is good with plenty of onions. To peel them easily, blanch them for a few minutes in boiling water, drain and remove the skins while they are still hot.

Serves 3–4

1 large rabbit, jointed
3 tbsp olive oil
675g/1½lb tiny (pickling) onions, peeled
5 ripe tomatoes, peeled and chopped
2–3 cloves garlic, chopped
2 bay leaves
5 cloves
1 tsp allspice
4 tbsp wine vinegar
salt and pepper

Fry the rabbit pieces in the oil until lightly browned all over. Then add the rest of the ingredients and simmer gently, covered, for about 1–1½ hours until the onions are very soft. Transfer to a serving dish and serve with rice.

CLAUDIA RODEN

Editor's note: A non-stick pan makes the frying easier and reduces the amount of oil you need. If the rabbit is done before the onions have become soft, remove it and set aside in a covered dish, returning it to the pan just to heat through and coat with the delicious, fragrant sauce. Though wholly unauthentic, a few frozen peas go well with this dish.

CHESTNUTS

Native to southern Europe, where they have been a regular part of the diet for centuries, and first introduced to Britain by the Romans, sweet chestnuts are the ideal accompaniment to any game dish. Their season lasts from October until just after Christmas, which coincides with the main game season. Most of those available here come from Spain, although they are also imported from Italy and France. Buy the best you can find – chestnuts can be time-consuming to prepare and second-rate ones have a high wastage rate. Look for undamaged nuts which are plump and feel firm. As a rule of thumb, 450g/1lb whole chestnuts will yield 225–340g/8–12oz of usable flesh.

For soups and stuffings the simplest way to deal with them, which avoids any peeling, is to cover them with water and simmer for 20–25 minutes until they feel soft in the centre when pierced with a knife. Slice in half down the middle, squeeze the skins gently and remove the chestnut flesh with a teaspoon. If you need whole chestnuts, simmer them for 8–10 minutes, taking them out of the water 2–3 at a time to peel. As long as they are hot, both the outer and inner bitter skin can be peeled off easily. Scoring them round the middle before you put them into the water makes the job slightly less fiddly.

Chestnut stuffing for game or duck

Parboil 45g/1½oz rice for 2–3 minutes in a covered pan. Cool, then mix with 85g/3oz cooked chestnut pieces, 30g/1oz pine nuts, 15g/½oz currants or sultanas, and ¼ tsp each of cayenne pepper and powdered cinnamon. Stuff the bird as usual.

LYNDA BROWN

Chestnut croquettes

Makes 9–10

Mash 2 slices of finely chopped ham with 225g/8oz cooked chestnut flesh to a stiff but creamy paste with a little cream or milk. Form into fat finger-shaped croquettes. Roll in breadcrumbs and let the breadcrumbs set – about an hour. Fry in a little vegetable oil for about 10 minutes, turning frequently, until brown and crisp. Serve with game or turkey.

LYNDA BROWN

Braised chestnuts with apple and cider

Serves 4

340g/12oz whole peeled chestnuts
300ml/10fl. oz cider
1 tsp sugar
1 medium Cox's eating apple, peeled, cored and
chopped into small neat dice
7–15g/¼–½oz butter for frying

Put the chestnuts in a single layer in a pan. Pour over the cider, add the sugar and simmer until soft, about 20–25 minutes. Remove the chestnuts to a serving dish, breaking them into large pieces. Boil down the juices to 2–3 tbsp and pour over the chestnuts. Fry the apple dice in a little butter for 2–3 minutes, and mix with the chestnuts. Serve with roast goose or game.

LYNDA BROWN

See also: Chestnut soup, p. 223.

WILD MUSHROOMS

Picking wild mushrooms: The main rule, when out looking for edible wild mushrooms, is: if you are in any doubt about identification, do not pick them. Always take a book with you, such as Roger Phillips' *Mushrooms & other Fungi of Great Britain & Europe* (Pan Books, £11.95). Photographs are much more helpful and have greater clarity than even the best colour illustrations, and this book comes with the date of photography as an extra guide. Even better, especially for a beginner, is to go with someone who has picked wild mushrooms before or join an autumnal Fungi Foray, organised by the British Mycological Society and other groups such as Cooking with Class Ltd, in Oxford. Real mushrooms do not always exactly match the photographs, and only experience can give you enough confidence to be absolutely sure that you are identifying a mushroom correctly.

When you are certain you have found a real chanterelle and not *Hygrophoropsis aurantiaca* (false chanterelle), which is edible but might give you hallucinations, or a real cep and not *Boletus luridus*, which can give you gastric upsets, check also that it isn't maggot-ridden. The best wild mushrooms are, in order of merit, the cep, the chanterelle, field and horse mushrooms, the blewit and the horn of plenty (or black trumpet).

Cultivated wild mushrooms: These are now available in the larger branches of most supermarkets, and in some greengrocers, and are obviously safer than picking them yourself. The most commonly found varieties are the *shiitake* (best cooked gently, in meat dishes that complement its strong flavour), the oyster mushroom (pale in colour and inclined to be slippery in texture, like its namesake), which is very good with fish or eggs, and the chestnut brown cap, or Paris brown, which looks like an ordinary white mushroom but firmer and with a brown top. It also has rather more flavour, and will withstand longer cooking, so is ideal in casseroles. In sophisticated outlets (Oxford market, for instance), you might also find chanterelles, ceps, *pieds de mouton* and horn of plenty. Check the 'use by' date, as all are very perishable, and use within 24 hours if possible. Cooked mushrooms and fungi freeze well.

Dried mushrooms and fungi: These are always worth buying, once you have checked that they are in fairly large pieces and aren't so old they have dried to a dust. They add a distinctive flavour to risottos and pasta dishes. They have to be soaked before using, and the water in which they soak can be used to add extra flavour to the dish. Look for brands from Italy and France, usually ceps (morels are also sold dried), and expect to

PARASOL MUSHROOM
LEPIOTA PROCERA

DRIED HORN of PLENTY
CRATERELUS CORNUCOPIOIDES

CHANTERELLE
CANTHARELUS CIBARIUS

MOREL
MORCHELLA ESCULENTA

OYSTER MUSHROOMS
PLEUROTUS OSTREATUS

CEP
BOLETUS EDULIS

99

pay a high price. They weigh light, however, and only 3–4 pieces can add a good deal to a risotto for 2 people. Those dried mushrooms sold in drums in supermarkets are only useful if you are sailing across the Atlantic, are short of space and willing to eat anything.

SIMONE SEKERS

Antonio Carluccio's cream of cep soup

Few people are ever likely to have a surplus of these highly prized mushrooms, except those in Scotland perhaps, where ceps are regularly to be found the size of soup plates. Adding even a few dried ceps to ordinary mushrooms in any kind of mushroom soup, however, as here, or to other dishes such as the one for veal chops that follows, will give you an idea of their distinctive meaty character and richness of flavour. Antonio Carluccio is a well-known mushroom culinary expert, and so I am pleased to be able to include this recipe, passed on by Thane Prince in one of her articles.

Serves 4–6

450g/1lb fresh ceps (*Boletus edulis*); or cultivated
mushrooms plus 30g/1oz dried ceps (*see* p. 98)
1 medium onion, finely chopped
4 tbsp olive oil
1l/1³/4pt beef stock
4 tbsp double cream
salt and pepper

If you are using dried ceps, soak them in lukewarm water for 10 minutes. Clean the mushrooms and cut them into pieces. Soften the onion in the oil for 3–4 minutes, then add the fresh mushrooms and sauté for 6–7 minutes. Add the stock, together with the dried mushrooms, if using, and their strained liquor, bring to the boil and simmer for 20 minutes if using fresh ceps, 30 minutes if using cultivated mushrooms and dried ceps.

Blend the soup in a blender or food processor until fairly smooth, return to the pan, add cream, salt and pepper and reheat slowly. Serve with croutons of bread fried in a little butter.

Veal chops with mushrooms and Marsala

Serves 2

2 thin loin veal chops
1 dsp olive oil and 7–15g/¼–½oz butter for frying
7g/¼oz dried ceps, rinsed and soaked in
85–110ml/3–4fl. oz boiling water for 15–30 minutes
(*see* p. 98)
55g/2oz mushrooms – puff balls, oyster, brown caps or
ordinary cultivated mushrooms – wiped clean and
chopped
60ml/2fl. oz Marsala
1 tbsp chopped chives
60ml/2fl. oz double cream

Seal the chops on both sides over a high heat in the oil and butter in a non-stick frying pan. Turn the heat down, cover, and cook gently for 3–5 minutes until the chops are just cooked. Turn off the heat and let the meat relax for 5 minutes to release its juices. Transfer the chops to hot plates and keep warm.

Meanwhile, finely chop the dried soaked mushrooms and add, with their soaking liquor, the fresh mushrooms, Marsala and chives to the pan juices. Cover and cook for 4–5 minutes until the mushrooms have softened. Add the cream, and boil down until the juices begin to thicken. Season to taste, remove the mushrooms to the plates and pour the sauce (there will not be much) over each chop. Serve with rice.

LYNDA BROWN

Italian olive and mushroom sauce for pasta

Of all the recipes I have had the pleasure of trying while compiling this book, this one from Claudia Roden (and the sweet and sour Venetian liver on p. 169) has excited me most. The paste from which the sauce is made has all sorts of possibilities: I have used it spread on croutes as an appetiser, to fill ravioli, thinned to make a sauce for polenta, and mixed with fromage frais to make a stuffing for pancakes. If using cultivated mushrooms, choose the large open-capped ones.

Serves 4

For the sauce
225g/8oz field mushrooms, wiped clean and thinly sliced
2 tbsp olive oil
1 clove garlic, crushed
170g/6oz pitted black olives (*see* p. 117)
3 tbsp chopped parsley
1/4 tsp or more chilli pepper (optional)
salt

To serve
450g/1lb tagliatelle
120ml/4fl. oz whipped double cream
55g/2oz fresh Parmesan

Lightly fry the mushrooms in the olive oil till soft, then blend in a food processor with the garlic, olives and parsley. Cook the tagliatelle until *al dente*. Meanwhile, heat the olive mixture, adding chilli pepper if liked and salt to taste. Mix with the tagliatelle and serve with a bowl of whipped cream and Parmesan.

CLAUDIA RODEN

See also: Italian mushrooms in oil, p. 192.

NETTLES

Rich in vitamins and mild in flavour, nettles at one time formed a regular part of our spring diet. Added to stews and vegetable broths, they were valued as a blood purifier and general promoter of health.

To avoid dirt and possible pollution from lead and car fumes, they should always be picked well away from roadside verges. Use only the young tender tips (the stems are invariably tough), snipping them off with a pair of scissors and wearing gloves to protect your hands. To prepare them, wash first in several changes of water to dislodge all the dirt (the tips have, in fact, hardly any sting to speak of and can, with care, be handled quite comfortably), then shake dry. If need be, they will keep for 2–3 days in a plastic bag in the refrigerator.

Nettle and spring onion soup

This makes an excellent springtime soup.

Serves 4

45–55g/1¹/₂–2oz tender nettle tops, well washed and
stripped from their stalks
150ml/5fl. oz each of milk and chicken stock or water
6–8 spring onions, green and white part, chopped
225g/8oz potatoes, peeled and diced

To finish
approx. 300ml/10fl. oz extra water, or milk and
water mixed
1 generous tbsp finely chopped spring onion
up to 15g/¹/₂oz butter

Simmer the first four ingredients in a covered pan until the potatoes are soft, about 15 minutes. Either mash with a potato masher to a rough purée or, if you prefer, blend until smooth and speckly. Dilute with extra water, adding a little more milk if you like, and bring back to the boil. Stir in the chopped spring onion, enrich with butter to taste and serve.

LYNDA BROWN

Nettle purée

Strip a good quantity of leaves from the stems and simmer for about 10 minutes in a large pan with a few tablespoons of water until softened but still bright dark green. Squeeze out the moisture and chop finely, either by hand or in a food processor, then return to the pan to dry off any excess moisture.

This basic nettle purée can be frozen or stored in the refrigerator for a few days in a covered container, and can be used in several ways: reheated with a lump of butter or crème fraiche and used as filling for omelettes; mixed into some creamy scrambled eggs and served with toast; puréed until smooth, seasoned and used as a base for poached eggs; mixed with thick cream to taste and used in small quantities as an accompaniment to chicken or veal; mixed with ricotta, seasoned with nutmeg and used as a stuffing for ravioli; or mixed with potatoes for a creamy potato and nettle purée.

LYNDA BROWN

ELDERFLOWERS AND HEDGEROW BERRIES

The elder (*Sambucus* sp.) is one of our most ancient native trees, and the creamy white clusters of elderflowers are a common sight in June in town and country alike. Their heady muscat fragrance will fill the house and kitchen in no time at all, and is one of the delights of early summer. The flowers can be used in a variety of ways to make fritters, to flavour syrups for summer fools and sorbets, to add to gooseberry pies, or to make elderflower vinegar to use with salads. And elderflower cordial does wonders for extempore fruit salads – see Simone Sekers' suggestions on p. 170. The trees bear their flowers over a month or so. Pick them well away from dusty roadsides, and shake them first to dislodge any insects. If you need to store them, put them into a plastic bag immediately, close the top and leave in the salad compartment of the refrigerator. They will keep in satisfactory condition for 2–3 days.

The sloe, or blackthorn, is the shrubby ancestor of the cultivated plum, and is widely found throughout the country in woods and hedgerows. Its small blue-black berries are borne on prickly branches and are picked in autumn (use gloves to protect your hands). They are too bitter to eat but can be turned into jelly and that admirable country warmer, sloe gin.

Other hedgerow berries worth gathering include those of the rowan and, of course, blackberries.

Salmon with elderflowers

Serves 4

1 tail end of salmon, approx. 675–900g/1½–2lb, filleted
generous handful elderflowers
150ml/5fl. oz dry white wine
60ml/2fl. oz water
salt and pepper

Wash the salmon, place the first fillet skin side down in an ovenproof dish, season and arrange the elderflowers in a layer along its length. Place the upper fillet on top, flesh side down. Tie with string or secure with cocktail sticks. Add the wine and water, season, cover with foil and bake in a hottish oven, 190°C/375°F/gas mark 5, for 20–25 minutes, or until the fish is just cooked. Serve with new potatoes. The cooking juices can be reduced by rapid boiling and enriched with a little double cream to form a sauce.

THANE PRINCE

Poached apples with elderflower syrup

Make a sugar syrup using 225g/8oz sugar to 600ml/1pt of water, and boil for 5 minutes. Infuse a handful of elderflowers in it for 1 hour, then strain through muslin and pour over peeled and halved Golden Delicious apples. Bake in a preheated oven, 180°C/350°F/gas mark 4, for 20–30 minutes, basting occasionally.

THANE PRINCE

Elderflower sorbet

Make a sugar syrup using 225g/8oz sugar to 850ml/1½pt of water. Add the juice of 2 lemons and a handful of elderflowers. Infuse as above. Strain through muslin and freeze in the usual way, stirring to break up the ice crystals once or twice as the sorbet hardens.

THANE PRINCE

Editor's note: A food processor makes excellent sorbets. Instead of stirring by hand, transfer the frozen syrup to the processor and whizz until creamy. Pile back into the container and freeze until required.

Elderflower cordial

Make a syrup using 1.125kg/2½lb sugar in 1.75l/3pt water, and boiling for 5 minutes. Pour into a deep bowl and stir in 55g/2oz of citric acid (available from chemists), 2 scrubbed and roughly chopped oranges and lemons, and about 20 large heads of elderflowers. Stir night and morning for 4 days, then strain through muslin. Bottle in sterilised bottles and store in a cool dark place (a refrigerator is good but not essential). To use, dilute 1 part cordial to 6 parts water, or to taste. This tastes wonderful mixed with fizzy mineral water, champagne or Pimms.

THANE PRINCE

Elderflower vinegar

Stuff elderflower heads into a bottle of good-quality wine vinegar or cider vinegar. Screw on the top and leave for a few days until the vinegar is well flavoured, replenishing with fresh flowers if necessary. Strain and use as required in salads – it is very good with avocado and pear salad, or cucumber and strawberry salad – vinaigrettes and sauces. Make other herb and fruit vinegars in the same way.

LYNDA BROWN

Sloe gin

Made in the autumn, sloe gin matures in time for Christmas.

approx. 450g/1lb ripe sloes
approx. 110g/4oz sugar
5–6 blanched, chopped almonds
1 standard bottle of gin plus 1 empty bottle

Pick over the sloes, discarding any rotten ones, and wash the fruit. Prick them well with a fork or a needle (or use 2 very short bursts in a food processor) so that the gin and juices can mingle. Half-fill the bottle with the sloes, add the sugar and almonds, pour on the gin to fill the bottle, and cork down. Store the gin for 3 months, shaking occasionally to help dissolve the sugar. Strain through muslin and rebottle.

THANE PRINCE

Joan Derby's hedgerow jam

This unusual and delicious dark jam was sent to Thane Prince by Joan Derby, a reader from Peterborough.

900g/2lb dark plums
1.125kg/2½lb sugar
285g/10oz elderberries
675g/1½lb blackberries
60ml/2fl. oz water
juice of 1 lemon
1 tbsp cider vinegar

Stone the plums and chop roughly, sprinkle with 225g/8oz sugar and allow to sit for 2 hours. Wash the elderberries and blackberries well, put in a pan with the water, and simmer gently until the fruit is very soft, about 15 minutes. Push the cooked fruit through a sieve or mouli and mix with the plums, lemon juice, vinegar and remaining sugar in a large pan. Bring to the boil, stirring gently while the sugar dissolves, then boil rapidly for 10–20 minutes or until the jam sets when tested. Pot and cover in the usual way.

THANE PRINCE

Rowan jelly

Rowan jelly is made in the same way as other jellies. The rowan tree, or mountain ash, is one of the most common ornamental trees in parks and roadside verges, as well as in the countryside, so there is never any difficulty in finding them. This is Simone Sekers' recipe. Sloe jelly is made in the same way.

Pick a good basketful of rowan berries when they are bright red – usually in September, or early October in the north. (Rowan trees prefer acid soil, and are just as likely to be found in the Surrey suburbs as in the uplands of northern England and Scotland.) Remove the larger pieces of stalk and leaves, but there is no need to string the berries from their finer stalks. Wash well, particularly if the crop is suburban. Put into a large preserving pan (preferably not aluminium), cover with water, bring to the boil and simmer until soft. Tip the contents of the pan into a jelly bag or an old, clean pillowcase and allow to drip into a deep jug or bowl overnight.

Next day, measure the juice and add 450g/1lb sugar per 600ml/1pt juice. Heat the sugar and juice slowly to melt the sugar, then bring to the boil. Boil rapidly to setting point (test on a saucer, to see when a spoonful will wrinkle when smudged with the tip of a finger). Pour into warmed, dry, clean jars.

This jelly never sets very firmly, but that means it melts more readily into any sauce or gravy. It improves with age, and a jar of vintage (5 years or more) rowan jelly is something to be treasured and served only to an appreciative audience.

SIMONE SEKERS

Eliza Acton's superlative redcurrant jelly

I include this recipe here because although it does not contain a hedgerow berry, it is the best and easiest recipe for redcurrant jelly I have come across. First published in 1845, in Eliza Acton's *Modern Cookery for Private Families*, the result is jewel bright and marvellously fruity. If the redcurrants are very dusty, wash them first, but there is no need to strip the stalks if you are short of time.

Run a thin layer of water over the base of a preserving or other large pan (preferably not aluminium: the acid in the fruit reacts with the metal, which is not desirable). Add an equal weight of redcurrants and sugar. Heat slowly, stirring until the sugar has dissolved. Boil for up to

8 minutes until a set is reached. Sieve the mixture into a bowl and pour the resulting liquid into small sterilised pots. Cover and seal as usual.

You will find that the actual boiling time necessary to produce a set varies with the quality and amount of fruit used as well as the size of the pan. It can be as little as 1 or 2 minutes for small quantities. Test with a spoon, as for rowan jelly (*see* p. 108). As soon as the last drop refuses to budge when the spoon is shaken, it is ready. Any scum will rise to the top of the pots and can easily be skimmed off.

For a slightly tarter jelly, which I prefer, reduce the sugar content by about 15 per cent. Pressing the debris gently against the sieve will yield more jelly which is not as clear but fine for general cooking purposes.

LYNDA BROWN

See also: Cumbrian hare, p. 93, and notes on game accompaniments, p. 84.

Blackberry and apple fool

This recipe comes from Myrtle Allen at the Ballymaloe Hotel in Ireland, where the hedgerows are thick with large juicy blackberries.

Serves 4–6

225–255g/8–9oz Bramley apples, peeled, cored and
sliced
30–55g/1–2oz sugar, or more to taste
340–450g/12oz–1lb ripe blackberries, fresh or frozen
120ml/4fl. oz double or whipping cream, whipped; or
thick beaten Greek yoghurt

Cook the apples with 1–2 tbsp water over a low heat until soft. Liquidise, then return to the pan to dry off any excess moisture. The purée must be very thick and dry. Sweeten to taste while hot, and leave to cool. Meanwhile, blend the blackberries to a thick pulp in a food processor, then sieve to remove the pips. Combine the blackberries and apple, mixing well. Fold in the cream or yoghurt and pile into individual glasses. Chill thoroughly for a few hours before serving.

A delicious autumn dessert, the blackberry and apple purée can be served as a compôte on its own, or served with yoghurt or thin pouring cream.

LYNDA BROWN

Blackberry and fromage frais tartlets

Serves 6

450g/1lb blackberries, washed
2–3 tbsp honey
1 tsp arrowroot, slaked in a little water
225g/8oz fromage frais or low-fat soft cheese
1 tsp rose-water
sugar to taste
6 x 7.5cm/3in shortcrust tartlet cases, baked blind
(allow approx. 225g/8oz prepared pastry)

Poach the blackberries with the honey and a dash of water. When they are tender, thicken the juices with the arrowroot to give a glossy sauce. Allow to cool. Beat the cheese with the rose-water and sweeten to taste. Just before serving, spoon the cheese into the tartlet shells and top with the blackberries.

THANE PRINCE

Al Fresco Eating

AL FRESCO EATING is lazy, informal, and full of the tastes and flavours of summer. Its main ingredients are plenty of fresh salads and vegetables, teamed with dishes that can be prepared in advance or cooked at the last minute. Above all, it is approachable food. Meat and fish dishes are kept simple, presentation unfussy and easy. Good bread is essential, and it is nice to have a few appetisers – a bowl of olives, *crudités*, tiny squares of Spanish omelette, and so on – to nibble and pick at with a glass of white wine as a prelude to the good things to come.

This kind of eating is very much to modern tastes, encompassing as it does the current vogue for barbecue food, popular now everywhere, and the enduring affection for that very British affair, the picnic.

It is clear from the Food and Drink pages of the last four years that al fresco cooking is something we take great pleasure in. The Mediterranean influence, predictably, is strong. No other culture quite captures the spirit of al fresco eating with such generosity, variety and flair. Just to smell rosemary smouldering over a charcoal fire conjures up memories of holidays spent in Provence or Tuscany. You will find many dishes throughout the book that lend themselves to this type of meal.

It is true: everything *does* taste better outdoors. As Claudia Roden wrote in her own book, *Picnic, The Complete Guide to Outdoor Food* (one of the best books on the subject), there is something about the fresh air and the liberating effect of nature which sharpens the appetite and heightens the intensity of sensations. Picnics have their own special magic, conjuring up memories of adventure and excitement, lazy hazy days spent in the countryside discovering hidden coves and open spaces, or stoically braving the weather, for, as it has been pointed out repeatedly, the British picnicker is the hardiest of species.

As people become more adventurous with food, so picnics, too, have developed far beyond sandwiches, tea and cake. Today's picnic is a riot of colour and flavour, with soups, different salads, savoury breads, spicy combinations and portable delicacies. The enormously popular annual Perfect Picnic competition run since 1989 by *The Daily Telegraph*, in conjunction with Krug Champagne, shows this clearly, and I have included a selection of my particular favourites from the finalists.

Prawn, pepper and coconut gazpacho

This mild, refreshing summer soup should be served very cold.

Serves 4

450ml/15fl. oz boiling water
170g/6oz finely grated fresh or desiccated coconut (*see* note below)
110g/4oz best-quality prawns, defrosted, drained on kitchen paper and coarsely chopped
1/2 green pepper, de-seeded and finely chopped
1 medium ripe tomato, peeled, de-seeded and cut into tiny dice
30g/1oz bulb fennel, finely chopped

Pour the boiling water over the coconut and leave to cool. Whizz briefly in a blender and then sieve, pressing hard to extract all the moisture from the coconut. This is the coconut milk. Stir in the remaining ingredients and serve well chilled in small iced bowls. (The coconut debris can be used in cakes.)

Note: Freshly grated coconut makes the best coconut milk. Grating the coconut is fiddly but can be done in advance and freezes well. This is how to do it:

Drain the liquid from a coconut, then smash it into pieces (a hammer is the best implement). Prise the white flesh away from the outer shell using a small sharp knife. This is easier if you heat the shell under the grill for a few minutes. Pare off the inner brown skin, rinse and pat dry, then process the lumps in a food processor until finely chopped – a matter of seconds. Use as above. It keeps beautifully in the freezer for 12 months or more. There is no need to thaw it first – just take out what you need with a spoon.

LYNDA BROWN

Melon and basil soup ⓥ

The quality of this delicious soup depends on the quality of the melon, so make sure you use a fragrant, full-flavoured one.

Serves 4

1 small very ripe melon, e.g. honeydew or charentais
15g/¹/₂oz basil leaves, stripped from their stalks
¹/₂ tsp sugar
approx. 150–240ml/5–8fl. oz mineral water
approx. 150ml/5fl. oz Greek yoghurt, or plain yoghurt
and cream mixed
2–4 tbsp sweet rich wine (optional)

First chop, then pound the basil to a sludgy paste with the sugar with a pestle and mortar. Process with the melon flesh and any juice squeezed from the melon skin in a blender or food processor until smooth, adding mineral water and yoghurt/yoghurt and cream until the taste and consistency seems right. Chill. Add wine if using, just enough to sharpen the flavour slightly, and serve immediately in small soup cups.

LYNDA BROWN

Iranian cold yoghurt soup ⓥ

Serves 6

850ml/1¹/₂pt plain yoghurt
150ml/5fl. oz sour cream
approx. 150ml/5fl. oz water
salt and pepper
1 cucumber, coarsely grated
4–5 spring onions, finely chopped
few sprigs of fresh mint, chopped
4 tbsp raisins or sultanas

Beat the yoghurt and sour cream with about 150ml/5fl. oz of water. Add the salt and pepper, cucumber and spring onions and stir well. Just before serving, put in six ice cubes and sprinkle with mint and raisins or sultanas.

CLAUDIA RODEN

Andalusian white soup with garlic and grapes ✓

This is another very easy and refreshing summer soup, known as *Ajo Blanco*, or 'white garlic', in Spain. Ground almonds make a perfectly good soup, but freshly ground whole almonds are better. It is also important to use fresh garlic.

Serves 6

200g/7oz shelled fresh almonds or ground almonds
200g/7oz day-old good white bread, crusts removed
milk for soaking (optional)
4 fresh garlic cloves, crushed
120ml/4fl. oz olive oil
600ml/1pt or more iced water
salt and 4 tbsp wine vinegar, or to taste
225–450g/8oz–1lb muscatel or other sweet grapes,
peeled and de-seeded

If you are using fresh almonds, boil them for 2–3 minutes. Drain and peel when they are cool enough to handle, then grind in a food processor. If you are using ground almonds, put them straight into the processor with the bread soaked in milk or water and squeezed dry, and the garlic. Blend to a smooth paste, adding the olive oil, drop by drop at first, through the feeder, then in a slow stream, as with mayonnaise. Finally, add sufficient iced water until the soup has a thick creamy consistency. Season with salt and vinegar, add the grapes and serve well chilled.

DIPS, SALADS
AND VEGETABLE DISHES

Olive and olivade anchovy paste (√)

Serves 6

110g/4oz pitted black olives
55g/2oz tinned anchovy fillets, drained
55g/2oz tin tuna, drained
pinch of allspice
4 tbsp cognac
2 tbsp olive oil
black pepper

This is one of the many spreads they call 'caviar' in Nice. Put all the ingredients in a food processor and blend to a smooth paste. Serve on small rounds of fresh bread or toast, allowing 2–3 per person.

CLAUDIA RODEN

Simone Sekers writes: OLIVES: It is odd that the hard, bitter fruit of the olive tree should produce one of the best seasonings. Green olives are the unripe fruit, treated to remove the bitterness by being immersed in brine. These can be flavoured with various herbs, or stuffed with peppers, almonds or anchovies. Black olives are the copper-coloured ripe fruit, and are blackened by their preservation process – again, these can be pickled with other flavourings, but are never stuffed. Olives in brine, in jars or tins, keep for some time and are essential store-cupboard items; of these the Fragata range from Spain is excellent. Those bought loose should be eaten at once since they dry out – check when you buy them that they look plump and enticing, and not dry and wrinkled, and taste one if you can to check that they haven't acquired the flavour of a neighbouring dish. One of my favourite ways of adding olives to a dish is to use olive paste, green or black depending on the food it is to accompany: Minasso Serafino produces a good one for the Culpeper shops, and I am particularly fond of Chalice Foods' Greek Olive Paste, available from health-food stores and from Selfridges. Use the paste in salad dressings, as a marinade for chicken and fish, as an instant pasta sauce (add extra olive oil), or dolloped on to pizzas, as a filling for cold omelettes, or simply on toast as an appetiser.

Baba Ghanoush Ⓥ

Serves 4

1 large aubergine
3 tbsp tahina
2 cloves garlic, crushed
juice of 2 lemons
2 tbsp water
salt
few sprigs of parsley, finely chopped, to garnish

This aubergine purée is popular all over the Arab world. Roast the aubergine under the grill, turning it a few times until the skin is black and blistered and the flesh feels very soft when you press it. Peel the aubergine and squeeze out the juice, then purée in a blender or food processor with the rest of the ingredients. Spread the cream on a flat plate and sprinkle with parsley. In the Arab world it is served with bread, but you may also serve it with *crudités*.

CLAUDIA RODEN

Editor's note: TAHINA is a nutty, creamy sesame-seed paste, widely used throughout the Middle East in salads and sauces. It is available in jars from most supermarkets, wholefood shops and delicatessens.

Salsa

Whatever did we do without salsa? This fiery Mexican dip, a mixture of chopped tomatoes, chillies and seasonings, used to accompany grilled chicken, beef or guacamole (see below), has taken the food world by storm over the last couple of years. The idea is brilliantly simple and can be adapted to produce any number of different (and not necessarily fiery) salsas, using chopped ripe tomatoes as the base with various other piquant additions. It has become my favourite dip to spoon over green summer salads. Here are two variations, the first from Claudia Roden and the second my own. (*See also* Thane Prince's beef and tacos with tomato and chilli salsa, p. 36.)

With guacamole: Very finely chop half a small onion, 1 or more small hot chilli peppers (stem and seeds removed), 3 ripe tomatoes and a bunch of coriander, using a food processor if you like.

Just before serving, dice the flesh of 2 medium ripe avocados, and season with lime juice and salt to taste, crushing the avocado a little with a fork (don't turn it into a purée). Serve the guacamole with the salsa for everyone to help themselves and mix the two to taste. Accompany with tortilla chips (*see* p. 37). Serves 4.

Summer salsa for green salads: Chop ripe tomatoes (allow 1–2 per person) by hand and put into a dish. Stir in a little finely chopped fennel, chopped capers, a splash of good wine vinegar, and a couple of tbsp of fruity olive oil. Season if necessary and add chopped herbs – tarragon, basil, mint, parsley, fennel tops, coriander – to taste. Use to spoon over green salads. Vary the salsa with chopped spring onions, avocado, black olives, garlic, anchovies or celery.

Carrot and potato appetiser ⓥ

This homely Tunisian appetiser is easy to make and full of spicy flavour. Serve it cold with bread.

Serves 6

675g/1½lb carrots
450g/1lb potatoes
salt
2 garlic cloves, chopped
4 tsp cumin
3 tbsp olive oil
2 tbsp wine vinegar
large pinch cayenne pepper

Peel the carrots and potatoes and cut them into pieces. Put them in a pan with the salt, garlic and water to cover, then boil until soft. Drain and mash, then stir in the rest of the ingredients.

CLAUDIA RODEN

Greek salad ⓥ

There is no better salad to eat out of doors than this, especially made with home-grown tomatoes and cucumbers. Make up one salad for each person in shallow soup plates rather than in one large dish. Arrange alternating slices of ripe tomatoes and cucumber in each bowl, slicing the cucumber thickly.

Allowing 30–45g/1–1½oz of feta cheese per person, slice into slivers, and arrange neatly on top. Dribble olive oil over and a squeeze of lemon juice if you like. Finish with a sprinkling of dried *rigani,* and scatter a few stoned and chopped black olives (*see* p. 117) over the whole. Serve with good bread and extra olive oil.

Note: Rigani is the dried wild marjoram from Greece, a much-used herb in the northern Mediterranean, and available in packets with other dried herbs and spices. At home, I use golden marjoram, *Oregano vulgare aureum,* from the herb garden (a pretty, hardy rockery plant) which is an excellent substitute. Chop it fairly finely, leave to dry for an hour or so and use as required. It will keep in this 'fresh dried' state for several weeks.

LYNDA BROWN

THE following four salads are suitable also for picnics. They can be made in advance and do not spoil. The first two are Middle Eastern.

Labnieh ⓥ

This is an Arab dish, found in Lebanon, Syria and Egypt.

Serves 6–8

225g/8oz shelled broad beans
450g/1lb basmati rice
4 tbsp olive oil
salt and white pepper
600ml/1pt plain yoghurt
1 tbsp dried mint
2 cloves garlic, crushed

Boil the beans briefly in salted water until tender, then drain. Wash and drain the rice, throw it into plenty of boiling salted water and let it boil vigorously for about 10 minutes. It should feel slightly hard when you bite it. Drain quickly and return to the pan. Stir in the olive oil and the broad beans, add salt if necessary and put the lid on tightly. Let the rice cook in its own steam over the lowest possible heat for another 15 minutes or until tender.

Beat the yoghurt and stir in salt and pepper, the mint and garlic. Let the rice cool and stir in the yoghurt mixture.

CLAUDIA RODEN

Bazargan

This cracked-wheat salad, writes Claudia Roden, comes from Syria. It keeps well and freezing does not spoil it: 'It must be prepared a few hours ahead and preferably overnight so that the wheat can absorb the dressing and become tender.'

Serves 15

450g/1lb burghul (cracked wheat)
2 large onions, finely chopped
150ml/5fl. oz olive oil
450g/1lb mixed chopped nuts such as walnuts,
hazelnuts, cashew nuts, almonds and pistachios
225g/8oz tomato concentrate
4 tbsp concentrated pomegranate syrup or tamarind
syrup, or the juice of 2 lemons
2 tbsp dried oregano (see p. 120)
2 tsp cumin
2 tsp coriander
1 tsp allspice
salt and pepper
55g/2oz parsley, finely chopped (optional)

Wash the burghul in a colander and soak in cold water for about 20 minutes, then drain. Soften the onions in 2 tbsp of the oil but do not brown Mix all the ingredients very thoroughly except the parsley. Leave, covered, in the refrigerator. Just before serving, stir in the parsley, if using.

CLAUDIA RODEN

Editor's note: Pomegranate syrup is the boiled down juice of a type of sour pomegranate and has a sweet-sour flavour. It can be bought from Middle Eastern and Greek stores, and some Indian grocers. Fresh pomegranates in this country are not suitable, as they are too sweet. Tamarind syrup is difficult to find in the UK, but you can use ordinary tamarind, which is readily available. For instructions on how to use, *see* p. 76.

Simone Sekers writes: BURGHUL is sold as bulghar, bulgar, pourgouri or cracked wheat, and is cooked wheat which is then dried and cracked between rollers. This means that it is able to absorb water with great ease, so it is enough merely to soak burghul if making a salad with it, as in this recipe. It can also be cooked, like rice, in pilafs. If you have a choice, pick the fine burghul for salads and the medium or coarse for pilafs. It is now widely available in supermarkets and wholefood shops.

Olive pasta salad ⓥ

Serves 6–8

2 red and 2 yellow peppers
340g/12oz pitted black olives (*see* p. 117)
2–3 cloves garlic, crushed
pinch of cayenne pepper
3 tbsp rum, or to taste
4 tbsp olive oil
450g/1lb spaghetti or spaghettini
salt
parsley, finely chopped, or basil, torn into pieces

Begin by roasting the peppers in the hottest part of the oven for about 30 minutes until they are brown all over, turning them once. Put them straight into a polythene bag, close it tightly and leave for about 10 minutes – this makes them easier to peel. While the peppers are still warm, peel them, pull the stems off, cut them open, remove the seeds, and slice the flesh into ribbons.

Mash the olives to a paste in a blender with the garlic, cayenne pepper and rum, then blend in the olive oil. Boil the pasta in salted water until barely tender and drain quickly. Put it in a bowl with the olive paste and mix well, then arrange the peppers on top. Serve sprinkled with parsley or basil.

CLAUDIA RODEN

Editor's note: This is a glorious pasta salad. If it is inconvenient to use the oven to roast the peppers, they may be put under the grill, turning them frequently until brown and blistered all over. Pasta shells or coils can also be used instead of spaghetti.

Oriental chicken salad

Serves 4

4 boneless skinned chicken breasts
bay leaf
slice of onion
carrot
stick of celery
1 small tin water chestnuts, drained and sliced into fine
matchsticks
3 pieces stem ginger (in syrup), sliced into fine
matchsticks
1¹/₂ tbsp sesame seeds

For the dressing
1¹/₂ tbsp soy sauce (*see* p. 130)
1 tbsp dry sherry
2 tbsp syrup from the stem ginger
1 tbsp wine vinegar
5 tbsp peanut or sunflower oil
pepper to taste

To finish
170g/6oz beansprouts
1 medium bunch spring onions
1 medium red pepper
85g/3oz Chinese thread noodles or similar pasta

Gently poach the chicken in water to cover with the bay leaf, slice of onion, carrot and stick of celery for 15–20 minutes until cooked, then allow to cool in the liquid for about 30 minutes.

Cut the chicken into 2.5cm/1in cubes and place in a large dish with the water chestnuts and ginger. Sprinkle with sesame seeds. Mix all the dressing ingredients together and pour one third over the chicken. Toss and leave in the refrigerator overnight.

To finish, rinse the beansprouts well, cut the onions into 7.5cm/3in strips and shred finely, slice the pepper likewise, cook the noodles according to the instructions on the packet, drain and reserve. Mix all the ingredients together with the reserved dressing and serve.

THANE PRINCE

Simone Sekers writes: ORIENTAL THREAD NOODLES are sometimes known as cellophane noodles and are usually made of mung bean flour. They should be soaked for about 10 minutes before cooking. If these are not available, use Chinese noodles instead, or one of the finer Italian pastas such as tagliarini or tagliolini.

THE following two salads are good to serve with traditional high teas, ham and meat salads, and buffet food.

Fresh pea and orange salad Ⓥ

Serves 4

225g/8oz fresh small peas (shelled weight) or frozen
petits pois
1 large orange, carefully peeled, de-pithed and chopped
3–4 sprigs fresh mint, chopped
1 dsp walnut oil
1 dsp balsamic vinegar (*see* p. 65)
salt and pepper

Bring some lightly salted water to the boil and cook the peas for three minutes, then refresh them by plunging into iced water. Drain, add the other ingredients and toss lightly.

THANE PRINCE

Blackcurrant beetroot Ⓥ

Serves 2–4

Make a sauce with 1–2 tbsp blackcurrant jam heated through with the juice of about half a lemon – it should taste sharply sweet. Pour over 2–3 small to medium roughly diced or sliced cooked summer beetroot. Serve in a fringe of lettuce leaves or with slices of cooked yellow beetroot around the edge.

LYNDA BROWN

Herb mayonnaises

Herbs added to mayonnaises are especially nice in summer and give a lift to ordinary mayonnaise, either the bottled kind or home-made. They can be used with numerous meat and fish dishes, as well as hard-boiled eggs or as a dressing for various salads. The secret is to pound the herbs to a paste first, rather than simply chop them. This results in a beautiful pale green speckled mayonnaise. Tarragon, sorrel, basil and fresh coriander make particularly good herb mayonnaises.

Strip the leaves from the stalks (remove the central mid-ribs from sorrel), chop, then pound with a pestle and mortar to a paste. Stir in mayonnaise to taste. To use, let down with a little hot water, a teaspoon at a time, to the desired consistency, and use as required. Or mix with thick creamy yoghurt to make a delicate sauce for fish or vegetable terrines and mousses, for avocado pears, cold poached salmon or chicken.

LYNDA BROWN

See also: Crab and courgette ramekins with basil mayonnaise, p. 64.

Poached salmon

A perfectly poached salmon, moist and succulent, served with mayonnaise, new potatoes and salad, is one of the great glories of summer eating. This is Thane Prince's foolproof method.

Wash the fish well and make sure all the kidney and the blood along the spine is removed. If this is not done the fish may be bitter. If you have one, or can borrow one, use a fish kettle (your fishmonger may rent or lend you one). Otherwise a large casserole can be used.

Simply place the fish in the kettle or casserole, cover with cold water, add 1 tbsp peppercorns, 2 tbsp salt, 2 bay leaves, some onion slices and a squeeze of lemon juice. Put the lid on and bring the water to the boil over a low/medium heat. When the water is about to boil, turn the heat down, let the fish simmer for 1 minute, then turn off the heat.

If you are serving the fish hot, let it sit in the water for 30 minutes; if serving it cold, leave it in the water until the fish has cooled.

THANE PRINCE

Escoffier's walnut and horseradish sauce for salmon and salmon trout

As a change from mayonnaise, this creamy sauce, which Escoffier first discovered on a visit to Savoie before the First World War, cannot be bettered. This is a lighter version than the original. If you prefer, you can use thick cream (up to 150ml/5fl. oz) instead of the yoghurt and cream mixture.

Serves 3–4

55g/2oz good-quality walnuts
5 tbsp each very thick Greek yoghurt and single cream,
beaten together
2 tbsp freshly grated horseradish (*see* p. 21)
1/2–1 scant tsp sugar plus lemon juice to taste

Pour boiling water over the walnuts, and pick off the skins as they become cool enough to handle. This is fiddly but the bitter taste of the skins would spoil the sauce. Chop very finely. Lightly mix with the rest of the ingredients, adding sugar and lemon juice to taste. Serve with cold poached salmon and trout.

LYNDA BROWN

Cider poached chicken with tarragon

A simple poached chicken is the other classic summer dish. This is a variation on the theme which produces perfect results every time. If you do not like cider, use a mixture of chicken stock, water and a glass of wine instead.

Serves 4–6

1.5kg/3¹/₂lb chicken
approx. 1.5l/2¹/₂pt each medium-dry cider and water
6–8 sprigs tarragon
12 green or black peppercorns

Make sure the chicken is thoroughly clean, and tie the legs loosely. Choose a pan into which the chicken will just fit comfortably. Bring cider, water, tarragon and peppercorns to the boil. Slip in the chicken, breast side up (if not completely immersed add extra boiling water). Cover and simmer over the lowest possible heat for 30 minutes: check that the liquid barely tremors. Turn off the heat and let the chicken cool in the liquid (3–4 hours), or leave until ready to eat.

Carve in the usual way, and decorate the slices with tarragon leaves. Serve with new potatoes, salad and the following cider-flavoured tarragon mayonnaise: boil down 300ml/10fl. oz of the poaching liquid to 2 tbsp, removing any scum. Beat into 150ml/5fl. oz mayonnaise, adding 1–2 tbsp chopped tarragon leaves, pounded to a paste first.

Note: The poaching liquid should not be wasted. Use it to simmer the carcass and any debris with a selection of chopped vegetables, bouquet garni and bacon rinds if you have some for 2–3 hours. Strain, cool and remove the fat. This enriched stock can now be frozen and used for soups and sauces.

LYNDA BROWN

BARBECUES

An Italian saying claims that 'even an old shoe tastes good if it is cooked over charcoal', and it is true that the method of cooking briefly, directly over glowing embers, imparts a unique flavour. The smell alone is most alluring.

Although it is the oldest form of cooking, the recent fashion for barbecuing came to us in the 1950s from the United States. It still bears the marks of America with its special equipment and accessories, bottled sauces, jargon rituals and organisation, and its casual informal style, in which the men do the cooking and the women the hostessing.

More recently, hamburgers and steaks have been upstaged by food from other countries, particularly from the Arab and Islamic world but also Indonesia, India, China and Russia, where grilling on charcoal has long been part of the way of life.

Barbecued foods are delicious *au naturel*, but the tradition of aromatics attached to cooking over a fire is worth exploring. Steeping meat in aromatic baths or marinades is a special refinement which tenderises it, helps to prevent it from drying out on the fire and impregnates it with flavour.

The following list of marinades for meat and chicken is only a tiny part of the huge variety which exists. Try one or more at a time, increasing the quantities as necessary. French gastronomic wisdom has it that salt should not go into a marinade as it draws out the juices, but I go along with most other cultures in leaving it in, finding that it makes no difference.

Buy tender meat like chops or steaks, or cut fillet or leg into 1/2–1in cubes. Use boned or jointed chicken (legs stay more moist and juicy), or cut it into cubes. Leave to soak in one of the marinades, covered, in the refrigerator overnight or for at least an hour, turning the pieces over a few times. Thread cubed meat on to skewers (the flat kind with twisted blades are best) or on to wooden saté or bamboo sticks.

The art of good grilling lies in making a good fire, distributing the heat evenly and controlling it by lowering or lifting the grill, which must be well oiled or the food will stick. You can use charcoal or wood (fruit wood and vine prunings impart a special flavour), but charcoal briquettes provide a longer, steadier, more intense heat. Start to cook only when the fire has burned down, the smoke has gone and a light powdery grey ash covers the glowing embers. Cooking must be done over gentle heat as flames will dry and scorch the food on the outside, leaving it uncooked on the inside. Brush the leaner, drier meats with oil or melted butter, and be careful not to overcook.
CLAUDIA RODEN

It is difficult to give cooking times since we all have different interpretations of rare, medium and well done, and it also depends on the thickness and type of food, its distance from the fire, the quality of the charcoal, the size of the firebed and the weather; so you need to test the meat's readiness by cutting through it with a sharp knife. Then all you will need to complete the meal is bread and salad, with fruit to follow.

The following quantities of marinade are sufficient for around 675–900g/1¹/₂–2lb meat.   CLAUDIA RODEN

Marinades for pork

Chinese: Mix 4 tbsp sesame oil, 4 tbsp dry sherry, 2 tbsp ginger juice, 2 crushed garlic cloves and salt. If you like, add 4 crushed cloves, ¹/₂ tsp cinnamon or aniseed and the peel of 1 dried tangerine, chopped.

Indonesian: Combine 4 tbsp sunflower oil, 4 tbsp soy sauce, 2 tbsp honey, 2 tbsp vinegar, 1 tsp aniseed, 2 crushed garlic cloves, 1 grated onion, salt and pepper.

Italian: Mix 4 tbsp olive oil, 2 tbsp wine vinegar, 1 tbsp fennel seeds, 2–3 crushed garlic cloves, salt and pepper.

Marinades for beef

French: For steak, mix 150ml/5fl. oz red wine with 4 tbsp olive oil, 2 bay leaves and pepper.

Indonesian: Mix the juice of ¹/₂ a lemon and 1 tsp tamarind paste (see p. 76), diluted with 2 tbsp water, 2 tbsp soy sauce, 1 tsp sugar, 3 crushed garlic cloves, 1 grated onion, salt and pepper.

Marinades for lamb

Indonesian: Mix 1 grated onion with 4 tbsp sunflower oil, 4 tbsp soy sauce, salt and pepper.

Italian: Mix 5 tbsp olive oil, 2 sprigs each chopped rosemary and sage, 4 crushed juniper berries, salt and pepper. This will also do for pork.

Moroccan: For brochettes, mix 5 tbsp oil, 2 tsp paprika, 1 tsp cumin, 1 tsp coriander, salt and a good pinch of cayenne pepper.

Turkish: For Turkish kebabs, mix 1 grated onion, 1 tsp allspice, 1 tsp cinnamon, 3 tbsp oil and salt.

Marinades for chicken

Creole: Mix 4 tbsp olive oil with 2 tbsp tomato purée, 2 crushed garlic cloves, a good pinch of hot chilli or cayenne pepper and the juice extracted from a 5cm/2in piece of fresh ginger.

French: Mix 150ml/5fl. oz dry white wine, 2 tbsp chopped tarragon and the grated peel of 1/2 scrubbed lemon.

Indian: For a tandoori chicken mix 5 tbsp yoghurt with 1 tbsp ginger juice, the juice of 1/2 a lemon, 2 crushed garlic cloves, 1 tsp ground cumin, 1 tsp ground cardamom, 1 tsp ground coriander, 1 tsp orange or red food colouring or 1 tbsp of paprika, salt and a pinch of cayenne or chilli pepper if you like.

Indonesian: Combine 4 tbsp dark soy sauce with 2 tbsp sherry, 2 tbsp ginger juice, 1 tbsp honey, salt and a pinch of ground chilli or black pepper.

Spicy Indonesian: Beat 100g/3^{1}/$_{2}$oz creamed coconut and 1 tsp tamarind paste (*see* p. 76) with 150ml/5fl. oz hot water and add the following ground spices: 1 tbsp coriander, 1 tbsp fennel, 2 tsp cumin, 2 tsp cinnamon and a good pinch of nutmeg. Beat well and add the seeds of 3 cardamom pods, 1 tbsp ginger juice, 1 grated onion and 2 crushed garlic cloves.

Japanese: Blend 4 tbsp soy sauce, 4 tbsp mirin (rice) wine or medium sherry, 2 tbsp oil and 2 tbsp sugar. You can also add a garlic clove and piece of fresh ginger, both crushed in a garlic press, and some grated orange or lemon zest.

Note: To make ginger juice, crush small peeled pieces of fresh ginger in a garlic press.

CLAUDIA RODEN

Simone Sekers writes: SOY SAUCE, SAKÉ AND MIRIN. Soy sauce is made from fermented soya beans and is a condiment much used in Chinese and Japanese cooking to heighten and underline the flavour of savoury dishes. There are many variations, each with its own character and flavour. Most easily available are those termed either 'thin' or 'light', which are generally less strong and salty than those labelled 'thick' or 'dark'. If using soy sauce, reduce the amount of extra salt you add to the dish.

Saké and mirin are both Japanese rice wines, with mirin a sweeter and more syrupy version of saké. Use dry or medium-dry sherry as a substitute for saké, and sweet sherry, or a mixture of dry sherry and honey, as a substitute for mirin.

Greek-style lamb kebabs

These are my favourite kebabs. The onion cooks to a delicious charred sweetness, and the bay leaves give off a wonderful aroma.

Serves 4

450g/1lb trimmed and boned leg of lamb, cubed into
2.5cm/1in pieces
1 onion, peeled, quartered and separated into layers
1–2 tbsp finely chopped fresh oregano; or 1–2 tsp dried
rigani (*see* p. 120), plus a little chopped fresh mint if liked
olive oil and lemon juice
bay leaves, fresh if possible

Put the lamb, onion and chopped herbs in a bowl, moisten lightly with olive oil, add a few drops of lemon juice, mix well and leave for an hour or so.

Assemble the skewers as follows: start with a slice of onion and a bay leaf, then a cube of lamb, then another slice of onion and a bay leaf. Repeat along the length of the skewer, finishing with onion, making sure you don't crowd the pieces and that everything is evenly spaced. Grill over charcoal (laying the skewers on sprigs of fresh rosemary if you have some) for approximately 10–15 minutes, turning occasionally. Serve with rice.

LYNDA BROWN

Marinated chicken breasts

Serves 4

4 large boneless, skinned chicken breasts
2 tbsp lemon juice
grated rind and juice of 1 large scrubbed orange
2 tbsp olive oil
salt and pepper
2 tbsp chopped fresh herbs (mint, thyme, parsley,
chives)

Wash the chicken and put into a shallow dish in one layer. In a bowl, mix the fruit juices, orange rind and olive oil, then season with salt and pepper. Stir in the herbs and pour the marinade over the chicken. Mix it thoroughly so that all sides of the meat are covered, and then refrigerate for 1 hour, turning the chicken once.

When you are ready to cook the breasts, grill them on the barbecue for 15 minutes, turning them once or twice and basting with the remaining marinade before you turn, to be sure the marinade is cooked.

THANE PRINCE

FISH barbecues as deliciously as meat. Not surprisingly, barbecuing was a popular theme in the hot summer of 1990 for *The Daily Telegraph* Perfect Picnic contest, judged at Blenheim Palace and attended by Thane Prince, whose article about the contest gave these two simple and memorable fish recipes from two of the finalists.

George and Ann Lloyd's barbecued scallops with Pernod sauce and jaca toast

Serves 4–8

16 large scallops with coral
seasoned butter, melted
French bread cut in 1.25cm/¹/₂ in slices

For the sauce
300ml/10fl. oz fish stock
150ml/5fl. oz white wine
75ml/2¹/₂fl. oz Pernod
juice of ¹/₂ lemon
salt and pepper
2 tsp chopped tarragon
few fine strips of orange and lemon peel, blanched for
4–5 minutes
150ml/5fl. oz single cream

First prepare the sauce: boil the stock, wine, Pernod and lemon juice until reduced by a third. Season to taste and stir in the tarragon and orange and lemon peel. Cool and take to the picnic in a lidded container. Warm the sauce on the barbecue, adding cream at the last moment.

Brush the scallops liberally with well-seasoned butter and grill for about 3–4 minutes each side. Serve on French bread toasted close to the coals for a few seconds, with a little sauce poured over.

Queelan Foo's barbecued salmon with ginger sauce

Serves 4

1 tail joint of salmon, filleted and descaled (approx.
20–23cm/8–9in long)
salt and pepper
vegetable oil for brushing

For the sauce
1 clove garlic, finely crushed
1 small piece fresh ginger, finely chopped
2 spring onions, chopped
2¹/₂ tbsp vegetable oil
1 tbsp light soy sauce
chopped fresh coriander

Season the salmon and brush with oil. Cook skin side down until the flesh is just opaque and the skin very crisp, about 10–15 minutes, depending on thickness, turning once. Mix the sauce ingredients together and warm on the fire. Serve the fish, sliced across, with the crisp skin and the sauce.

THANE PRINCE

Barbecued bread (√)

Baking flat breads – pittas – on the barbecue is easy and fun: the outsides become charred here and there in a most appetising way. They are marvellous with sausages grilled on the barbecue dunked in aioli, or to accompany vegetable side-dishes and salads to nibble at while the meat or fish is cooking. Any everyday bread recipe, brown or white, is suitable. Allow it to rise in the usual way, then simply break off small portions of dough, roll them out into oval shapes, about 1.25cm/¹/₂ in thick on a floured surface, and leave until you're ready to cook the bread. Lay them on the barbecue grill well away from the coals (otherwise you risk charring them too much before the insides have cooked properly) and cook for 2–3 minutes either side, turning once they have puffed up, which they usually do in a spectacular fashion. As an alternative to home-made dough, Thane Prince suggests using a packet of bread mix made up according to the instructions, then cooked as described above.

LYNDA BROWN

Barbecued vegetables ✓

Eating food cooked over the barbecue is so much part of our everyday life during summer that I am often more than content to have vegetables grilled over the barbecue instead of meat or fish. Either thread them on skewers to make kebabs, alternating with slices of onion, fresh bay leaves or sage, and perhaps cooking them over sprigs of rosemary, or simply lay them on the barbecue, whole or sliced as appropriate, painted with olive or spiced chilli oil, and perhaps sprinkled with fennel seeds, and turn them until they are browned and cooked.

A wide range of vegetables is suitable: courgettes, corn on the cob, peppers, aubergines, fennel, cauliflower, tomatoes, carrots, mushrooms, mange-touts, baby onions, globe artichokes (cut into 4 or 6 wedges, remove the choke and central leaves, rub with lemon and paint with olive oil, and cook slowly for 30–40 minutes), even fat fresh cloves of garlic. Scrubbed and parboiled unpeeled potatoes, cut into thick chunks, oiled and seasoned, are a revelation cooked on the barbecue – an idea I picked up in Portugal – and one of the best accompaniments to barbecued meat.

For vegetarians, you can make kebabs with a selection of vegetables and cubes of tofu (marinated first, for example, in one of Claudia Roden's suggestions on p. 129); or mix vegetables and fruit such as wedges of pineapple; or add a few cubes of bread, oiled and rubbed with garlic or rolled in herbs, which give a crisp contrast.

Except for soft vegetables like mushrooms or tomatoes, vegetables take longer to cook than meat or fish which is generally cooked briefly, so allow for this when planning the order of cooking. Make sure, too, when making kebabs, that you choose vegetables which will cook in about the same time. If you want to include very hard vegetables like carrots or cauliflower, blanch them briefly first.

As with meat, there are no hard and fast rules about marinades or cooking times: depending on the vegetable they can be as soft or crisp as you like. In any event, cooking times are rarely critical – let experience and common sense be your guide.

As a main course, rice is the best accompaniment to vegetable kebabs. A big handful of chopped fresh summer herbs, or a pat of your favourite savoury butter, stirred into the rice just before serving is delicious. Or try the basil, tomato and anchovy relish below. Creamy sauces are out of place for barbecued food. Choose instead dips and relishes based on Mediterranean flavourings to accompany the vegetables. Best of all is a pot of aïoli (*see* p. 136), made with fresh 'wet' garlic available from June onwards. It is the perfect accompaniment to all barbecued food, be it meat, fish or vegetables.

Note: For chilli-spiced oil, frizzle 2–3 dried chillis in a small amount of olive or vegetable oil. Use to brush vegetable kebabs or fish.

LYNDA BROWN

Barbecued corn on the cob ⓥ

Remove the silks (brown tufts) and husks of the cobs and turn over a gentle fire for 15–20 minutes until they are well browned, with black spots outside and milky tender inside. Serve with salt, coarsely ground black pepper and plenty of butter.

Another method is to pull down the husks, remove the silk and soak the husks in water for a few minutes so that they will not burn. Pull them up again, twist them closed and grill over hot coals for 20–25 minutes, turning occasionally. This way the corn stays pale yellow.

The corn husks can be used for wrapping round small and medium-sized fish grilled on the barbecue. Soak them in water for a few minutes and tie them up at the silk end with the fish inside. They can go straight on to the bed of coals. Turn them over once, allowing 15 minutes for a medium-sized fish.

CLAUDIA RODEN

Basil, tomato and anchovy relish

Combine 1 largish, peeled, very ripe tomato with a handful of basil leaves and 1 anchovy in a food processor or blender with enough olive oil to make a very thick sauce. Use as a dip for crudités, a sauce for grilled or barbecued fish, or to stir into cooked hot rice. Sufficient for 2–3 small servings.

LYNDA BROWN

Aïoli

For barbecued meat and fish, poached cod, and cooked summer vegetables such as cauliflower, carrots, potatoes, artichokes, broad beans and French beans, for spreading on dry croutes to float into fishy broths, there is nothing finer than aïoli, the fabled, pungent and addictive garlic mayonnaise from Provence. No grilled steak or sausages on the barbecue at home would be complete without it. The best aïoli is undoubtedly made from newly harvested fresh 'wet' garlic which arrives in the shops from late May. Mild and juicy, and far more digestible than garlic dried for keeping, this can be mashed easily to a heady garlicky pulp which, when combined with eggs and olive oil, produces a completely different result from chopped garlic simply stirred into ordinary mayonnaise. The other essential ingredients are good fresh eggs (the deeper the yolk colour the better, producing a sunshine golden mayonnaise) and a strong and fruity extra-virgin olive oil.

The amount of garlic can be altered to suit, but it should be a generous quantity. Some people like to include a little lemon juice, though I much prefer the pure taste of garlic, eggs and olive oil. Use the quantities given below as a guide, adding olive oil until the taste seems right. Aïoli will keep for a few days, covered in the refrigerator. As with ordinary mayonnaises, if it starts to curdle, start again with another egg yolk, and then add the curdled mayonnaise a little at a time, beating well after each addition. When this is all incorporated, add the rest of the olive oil. A little hot water – 1–2 tbsp, depending on the quantity of mayonnaise you are making – stirred into the curdled mayonnaise usually rectifies matters also; but if you remember to have everything at room temperature and to add the oil drop by drop to begin with until an emulsion has formed, there should never be any problem.

Serves 4

4–6, or more, fresh fat cloves of garlic
1/4–1/2 tsp salt, or to taste
2 fresh egg yolks
up to 300ml/10fl. oz olive oil
a little lemon juice (optional)

Using a pestle and mortar, mash the garlic cloves with the salt to a creamy paste. Stir in the egg yolks, beating well. Add the oil, drop by drop at first, amalgamating it well after each addition. Once an emulsion has formed it can be added in a slow trickle, again beating well until it becomes, as was once memorably described by Elizabeth David, a thick 'golden shining ointment'. Check for seasoning, adding a few drops of lemon juice if you like as you go along.

Note: Aïoli can also be very successfully made in a smaller quantity using 1 egg yolk, reducing garlic and oil proportionally.

LYNDA BROWN

Barbecued fruit

Once the meat and vegetables have cooked, the best way of taking advantage of the lingering fire is to barbecue fruits. Here are a few tasty suggestions taken from Claudia Roden's own book on outdoor food, *Picnic: The Complete Guide to Outdoor Food.*

Caramelised apples: Stick hard eating apples on the end of a skewer and hold them very close to the fire, turning them until the skin blisters and comes off easily, about 8 minutes. Drop into a bowl of sugar and return to the fire until the sugar melts and caramelises.

Bananas: Bananas cook very well in their skins. A Creole way is to slit them open and press in 1 tsp each of sugar and rum and a sprinkling of cinnamon. Put them on the grill for 10 minutes, turning once.

Editor's note: Bananas cooked this way (you can do the same thing by placing them under a domestic grill), even plain and done without opening their skins, become soft and luscious and acquire a delicious honeyed sweetness. Always choose ripe spotty bananas when you can.

Oranges with rum: Peel large oranges, removing the pith. Cut into slices and re-form, sprinkling with a very little brown sugar and cinnamon. Wrap in two layers of foil to prevent leakage, sprinkling a little rum inside, and put on the fire for 10–15 minutes.

Mixed fruit skewers: Thread alternate pieces of fruit such as quartered peaches, halved apricots, 2.5cm/1in chunks of unripe banana slices, chunks of pineapple, orange segments, apples and pears cut into wedges and sprinkled with lemon juice to prevent browning, pitted plums or cherries. Cook over a medium fire, turning for 5–10 minutes. Sprinkle with sugar and let them caramelise over the fire.

Alternatively, brush frequently with 110g/4oz melted butter mixed with 1 tbsp sugar and 1 tsp cinnamon, powdered ginger or the seeds from a cardamom pod. Or you can squeeze orange or lemon juice into the butter. Serve with a little of the basting sauce poured over.

CLAUDIA RODEN

PICNICS

The golden rule for picnics in our unpredictable climate is to include at least one dish that can be heated or chilled according to the weather. Soup is usually the easiest (see Thane Prince's suggestions below), but rolls or quiches can be kept warm in insulated bags, and many cold chicken or ham dishes can be served hot from wide-necked Thermos flasks. Another maxim I follow is never to take coffee in a Thermos, but to fill the Thermos with boiling water instead, and take a jar of really good instant coffee – Nescafe's Alta Rica or Cap Colombie – that can be made on the spot. Accompany this with some good plain chocolate (Bendick's Sporting & Military, Waitrose Continental or Sainsbury's cooking chocolate) and it will taste even better.

Unless you are having a proper table-and-chairs picnic, do take food that really can be eaten with a fork, and from plates that don't bend. Trying to cut a slice of rare roast beef with the side of a fork on a paper plate is bound to end in disaster, and lots of left-over beef. A salad of large lettuce leaves can be difficult to eat one-handed too; it is much easier to serve quarters of Little Gem lettuce that can be dipped into a vinaigrette or mayonnaise and then eaten with the fingers. And don't spurn the humble sandwich: try a filling of fromage frais and lumpfish caviar in thin slices of brown bread to serve with hot or iced consommé, or cream cheese and chives in rye bread to eat with smoked salmon, both of which are easy to eat, sustaining and elegant.

If you are keen on picnics, it makes sense to have a complete picnic kit at the ready, so that indispensable items such as salt and pepper, corkscrew and napkins are always to hand and not forgotten in the general rush. Paper napkins are fine, but it is a good idea to pack a damp flannel or two in a polythene bag, or a plastic bag of baby wipes. And take spare polythene bags to hold dirty plates and cutlery on the homeward journey.

SIMONE SEKERS

Lettuce and pea soup

Serves 4–6

1 medium lettuce, shredded
225g/8oz garden peas, shelled weight
1 shallot, finely chopped
1 tbsp light vegetable oil
3–4 sprigs tarragon, plus a few extra leaves for
decoration
600ml/1pt good chicken stock
salt and pepper

To finish
150ml/5fl. oz single cream

In a large saucepan, gently fry the shallot in the oil until transparent. Add the shredded lettuce, peas and tarragon. Stir everything well, pour in the stock and simmer for 10–15 minutes. Either liquidise and sieve the soup, or push through a mouli to remove the pea skins. Season well and allow to cool. If serving cold, stir in the cream just before serving and top with a few leaves of extra tarragon. If serving hot, reheat to boiling, add the cream and serve at once.

THANE PRINCE

Carrot, apple and cardamom soup ⓥ

Serves 4

225g/8oz carrots, peeled
225g/8oz cooking apples, peeled and cored
1 tbsp olive oil
1 Spanish onion, finely chopped
crushed seeds from 4 cardamom pods
1. 5cm/2in cinnamon stick
600ml/1pt vegetable or chicken stock
salt and pepper
grated nutmeg (if serving hot)

Heat the oil in a saucepan and fry the onion until soft. Add the carrots, apples and spices and cook, stirring, for 2–3 minutes. Add the stock, bring to the boil, cover the pan and simmer for about 20 minutes or until the carrots are tender. Liquidise in batches. (You may leave in the cinnamon stick.) Return to the pan, taste to correct the seasoning, adding salt, pepper and extra water if necessary. Serve either hot or cold. If serving hot, grate a little fresh nutmeg over the surface of the soup.

THANE PRINCE

NOWHERE is more associated with English picnics at their stylish best than Glyndebourne, the setting for the judging of the first *Daily Telegraph*/Krug Champagne Perfect Picnic competition in 1989, which produced some stunning and colourful entries and included dishes such as potted langoustine with ginger and dill, guinea fowl basted with quince jelly, monkfish with saffron mayonnaise, broad bean salad flavoured with fresh herbs and roasted cumin and coriander – plus some delightful watercress and walnut sandwiches, made with slices of pumpernickel bread spread with a mixture of chopped fresh watercress, Greek yoghurt and low-fat soft cheese, and topped with walnut halves fried in butter until crisp.

Simone Sekers was there to record the event for the Food and Drink page, and Claudia Roden was one of the judges. The following two recipes are from the winner, Brian Glover (whose cardamom cake appears on p. 14), and another finalist, Yu Yasuraoka-Finch, who prepared a Japanese feast with a sesame-seed theme.

Brian Glover's wild rice salad (√)

Serves 4

For the dressing
7 tbsp olive oil
juice and rind of 1 scrubbed lemon
6 spring onions
handful chopped parsley and fennel tops
salt and pepper

140g/5oz cooked wild rice
1 tbsp capers, chopped
55g/2oz currants
1 bulb fennel, chopped fairly small
1 clove fresh garlic, finely chopped (optional)
55g/2oz toasted pine nuts

141

Use 5 tbsp of oil and 2 tbsp lemon juice to make a dressing with the spring onions and herbs. Season. Dress the rice while still warm, adding the capers and currants. Fry the fennel for 2 minutes in the remaining oil, add garlic if using and cook for 1 minute longer over a low heat so that it does not burn. Add these to the rice, mix and adjust seasoning if necessary. Add the pine nuts just before serving.

Simone Sekers writes: GARLIC is now very popular, particularly when used properly (cooked slowly, whole, and not added indiscriminately in the form of acrid garlic salt, or crushed in a garlic squeezer). This salad is better for it (but not at the dinner interval at Glyndebourne, when your next-door neighbour in the stalls might not have had it). If you want just a suspicion of garlic flavour, crush rather than chop the garlic, cook it gently with the fennel for a minute, then remove.   SIMONE SEKERS

Yu Yasuraoka-Finch's five tastes baked omelette

Don't be tempted, warns Simone Sekers, to use fresh crab for this recipe, as the flavour will be too pronounced.

Serves 4–6

30g/1oz mange-touts, topped, tailed and sliced
55g/2oz sliced mushrooms
butter and vegetable oil for frying
6 eggs
3 dsp saké (*see* p. 130) or dry white wine
3 dsp sugar
1/2 tsp salt
1 2.5cm/1in long piece of carrot, grated
170g/6oz tinned crabmeat
1/2 box salad cress

Preheat the oven to 180°C/350°F/gas mark 4 and heat a lightly greased 18 x 10cm/7 x 4in loaf tin in it. Fry the mange-touts and mushrooms in a little butter and oil in a non-stick frying pan until just tender. Beat the eggs with the saké or wine, sugar and salt. Add all the other ingredients, including the liquid from the tin of crab. Return this mixture to the pan and cook until just beginning to set, scraping the bottom of the pan to prevent the mixture from sticking. Transfer to the heated loaf tin and cook until firm, about 30–35 minutes. Turn out carefully and leave to cool before cutting into bite-sized pieces.   SIMONE SEKERS

Gravetye's fresh herbed ham hock and lentil salad

This recipe comes from the celebrated Gravetye Manor hotel and restaurant near East Grinstead, and is a good example of how inexpensive ingredients can be turned into something out of the ordinary. It can be made in advance, freezes well and is worth making in quantity. Presoaking the lentils means they cook very quickly. Star anise, an attractive small chestnut-brown star-shaped spice, imparts the marvellous aromatic quality to the lentils in this dish, and is available from Chinese supermarkets, delicatessens and wholefood shops.

Serves 4–6

1 large ham hock, approx. 1–1.25kg/2¼–2½lb,
soaked in water for 24–36 hours
1 onion, finely chopped
1 carrot, chopped
1 stick of celery, chopped
2 cloves garlic, crushed
6 peppercorns
bouquet garni – bayleaf, parsley, thyme
110g/4oz green lentils, soaked in water 3–4 hours
1 carrot, diced
½ small onion, finely chopped
1 star anise

To serve
2–3 tbsp mustard vinaigrette
chopped fresh herbs – selection from chervil, tarragon,
parsley, chives, thyme and mint as available
mixed salad leaves
a few cherry tomatoes (optional)

Put the ham hock, chopped vegetables, garlic, peppercorns and bouquet garni in a large pan, cover with water and simmer very gently for around 2½ hours, or until the meat begins to part easily from the bone. Cool in its stock, which should jellify.

Drain the lentils, and cook with the carrot, finely chopped onion and star anise with enough of the ham stock to cover until just tender, about 5–10 minutes. Cool.

Discarding all skin, fat and gristle, take the meat from the bone and dice neatly into bite-sized pieces. Make a little thick mustard vinaigrette in the usual way, using powdered English mustard, a little finely shredded onion or shallot and a generous helping of fresh herbs.

Drain the lentils if necessary of any excess liquid. Lightly combine the lentils and ham, moistening with vinaigrette (the salad can be packed in a box at this stage for taking on picnics). Serve on a bed of salad leaves, decorated with cherry tomatoes if liked.

The cooked ham hock will keep up to a week in the refrigerator covered in its jellied stock. Strain and boil down further if it has not quite set to a jelly first. Any leftover stock makes delicious dried pea, lentil or vegetable soups.

LYNDA BROWN

Oven-fried Parmesan chicken

Serves 4–6

4 chicken breast fillets
1 tbsp Dijon mustard
3 tbsp olive oil
1 tbsp lemon juice
30g/1oz Parmesan cheese (*see* p. 197), grated
55–85g/2–3oz fresh breadcrumbs
a little garlic salt

Slice the chicken breasts into 4–5 strips. Marinate these in the mustard, oil and lemon juice, well mixed, for 30 minutes. Mix the cheese, breadcrumbs and garlic salt in a dish and coat the chicken strips, one at a time, pressing the coating on well (a spatula is best).

Lay the strips on a non-stick baking sheet, drizzle with a little more oil and bake in a preheated oven, 220°C/425°F/gas mark 7, for about 20 minutes, turning occasionally until browned on all sides. Cool on a rack to drain off excess oil. Serve with a bowl of garlicky mayonnaise (aïoli) and crudités.

THANE PRINCE

Honey-roasted quail

Serves 4

4 oven-ready quail
salt and pepper
2–3 tbsp olive oil
1 shallot, finely chopped
180–240ml/6–8fl. oz wine
4 fresh sage leaves
1 dsp honey

Wash and dry the quail and season with salt and pepper. Heat the oil in a frying pan which has a lid and brown the quail on all sides. Remove from the pan and brown the shallot. Put back the quail, pour over the wine, add the torn sage leaves, cover and simmer for 20 minutes. By then the quail will be cooked. Add the honey to the cooking juices, stir to dissolve, turn up the heat and boil until the juices begin to caramelise and thicken to a glaze. Baste the birds and place on a dish. Spoon over the honey glaze and serve cold.

THANE PRINCE

Editor's note: The wild rice salad on p. 141–2 and the fresh pea and orange salad on p. 124 are good accompaniments.

Fillet of beef with tarragon

Serves 6

675g/1½lb fillet of beef (trimmed weight)
2 tbsp olive oil for cooking
salt and black pepper
6 tbsp virgin olive oil
lemon juice to taste
handful of fresh tarragon, chopped

Heat the oven to 250°C/475°F/gas mark 9. Pour the olive oil over the meat, season well with black pepper and roast in the oven for 30 minutes. Remove and allow to cool.

When the meat is cold, slice it fairly thinly and cut these slices into strips (this makes the beef much easier to eat at your picnic). Pour the virgin oil over the beef and add the lemon juice to taste. Season with salt and pepper and mix in the chopped tarragon. Allow at least 3–4 hours for the meat to take up the flavours of the sauce.

THANE PRINCE

DESSERTS

Soup of red fruits

This delicious French dessert, writes Thane Prince, is quick to make and keeps well in the refrigerator. Serve with cream or Greek yoghurt. Try to use at least four types of berries, using the measurements given as a guide.

Serves 6–8
¹/₂ bottle red wine
1.5kg/3lb assorted red fruit – redcurrants, blueberries,
blackberries, blackcurrants, raspberries, cherries or
strawberries
approx. 170g/6oz sugar or to taste

Put the wine into a large saucepan and add all the fruit that needs cooking: currants, blackberries, blueberries and cherries. You can use either fresh or frozen fruit, whatever is available. Dissolve the sugar in the mixture, sweetening to taste, and allow the mixture barely to simmer for 4–5 minutes. Remove from the heat and let it cool before adding the strawberries and raspberries. Pour into a glass serving bowl and refrigerate until needed.

THANE PRINCE

Devon junket

It is easy to forget how good this simplest of desserts can be. Cool, slippery, light and creamy, it is perfect on a hot sunny day for eating out of doors with summer fruits and compôtes. It is important to make it with the creamiest milk you can buy. At home, I make it with unpasteurised (green top) milk, which is still available in some rural areas.

Commercial rennet has added almond flavouring, which gives the junket a hint of extra flavour. When I first published the recipe, many readers wrote to enquire where they could buy rennet. Supermarkets and chemists usually stock it. The main supplier (of Stone's Essence of Rennet) is Ernest Jackson & Co. Ltd of Crediton, Devon, who supply a recipe leaflet and help with stockists if needed.

Heat the milk to blood heat (39°C/100°F). For each 600ml/1pt of milk, stir in 2 tsp of rennet and 1 tbsp of sugar. Pour into a glass bowl and leave in a warm place to set, about 15 minutes. Serve well chilled, plain or sprinkled with freshly grated nutmeg. Serves 2–4

LYNDA BROWN

Majorcan ice-cream (gelat d'ametilla)

This is the most famous of Majorcan ice-creams. It is actually a sorbet and is ideal served with fresh cherries or a fresh apricot, strawberry, raspberry or blackcurrant coulis.

Serves 8

255g/9oz blanched almonds, finely ground (use a food
processor)
285g/10oz sugar
1l/1³/₄ pt water
finely grated zest of 1 scrubbed lemon
small stick cinnamon

Put all the ingredients in a pan over a low heat. Bring to the boil, stirring frequently. As soon as the mixture boils, turn off the heat and leave to cool. Remove the cinnamon. Either pour into an ice-cream maker and churn in the usual way, or pour into a container and freeze. Once frozen, process to a smooth cream in a food processor and refreeze until required. Allow to soften in the refrigerator for 15 minutes before serving.

LYNDA BROWN

Brian Glover's cardamom cake with apricots and white currants

Brian Glover, winner of the second Perfect Picnic competition, introduced this simple but magical cake. Very moist and light, it is best made 24 hours in advance. If white currants and apricots are not available, suggests Simone Sekers, try any mixture of sharp and sweet fruit to achieve the same balance.

Serves 6

For the cake
110g/4oz butter
85g/3oz vanilla sugar
2 eggs, beaten
rind and juice of 1/2 scrubbed orange

200g/7oz fine semolina
100g/3¹/₂oz ground almonds
1 tsp ground cardamom
2 tsp baking powder

For the topping
450–675g/1–1¹/₂ lb fresh apricots, halved and stoned
225g/8oz punnet white currants, cleaned
scant 300ml/10fl. oz water
110g/4oz caster sugar
1 vanilla pod
3 crushed cardamom pods
juice of 1 orange

To make the cake, cream the butter and vanilla sugar together, beat in the eggs and orange rind, then the semolina, almonds, cardamom and baking powder. Fold in the juice. Bake in a lined 20–23cm/8–9in tin at 190°C/375°F/gas mark 5 for 30–40 minutes.

Meanwhile, make a syrup with the water, sugar, vanilla and cardamom pods, and orange juice. Taste and remove the cardamom pods when the flavour is strong enough. Poach the apricots until tender but not collapsing, then remove with a slotted spoon. Poach the white currants for 1–2 minutes only, scoop out and allow to drain. Remove the vanilla and cardamom pods, pour the syrup over the cooked cake and allow to cool. Arrange the fruit on top of the cake, and leave for 24 hours if possible before serving with a mixture of Greek yoghurt and whipped cream.

SIMONE SEKERS

See also: Ricotta ice-cream, p. 210; Apricot ice, p. 209; Coffee granita, p. 209.

Impromptu Food

WHEN I WAS first writing out my notes for this chapter, I jotted down: 'No oven, chilling, marinading, etc. Just take food (fresh and store cupboard), cook and eat.' It became a good working definition of the kind of recipe I would most appreciate being able to turn to at any time when an impromptu meal was called for, or for when I wanted to produce something good to eat quickly from whatever happened to be at hand, and which wouldn't require too much preparation or thought.

There was a time when any kind of fast food meant opening a tin or packet, but as the quality and variety of foods available have increased, and tastes have become simpler, impromptu eating has taken on a whole new and exciting dimension. With a well-selected larder, a few prime (not necessarily expensive) ingredients, and a little ingenuity, a nourishing dinner can be made in no time at all. The result is colourful, cheerful, satisfying food, all the better for responding to the needs of the moment. Modern technology in the form of food processors takes out the hard work and speeds up the process enormously. Make a simple salad or vegetable starter, offer fresh fruit for dessert and the meal is complete.

THE ESSENTIAL STORE CUPBOARD

In the sixteenth and seventeenth centuries, a housewife was judged by the quality and delicacy of the provisions she laid down in her still room and cellars. These were used, especially in winter but throughout the year, not just as a means of thrift and preservation, but to add variety to the daily diet. A modern store cupboard fulfils the same function, except that we now have a much wider variety of ingredients from which to choose. Here are Simone Sekers' suggestions of indispensable items to have at hand:

Tins of tuna in brine; anchovies in oil; tinned tomatoes, beans and chickpeas (much quicker than using the dried sort, but as they are canned with added sugar for some reason in this country, rinse them well before use); condensed consommé; olives in brine; fruit in natural juice (not syrup).

Dried pasta (of all shapes); brown (or preferably green) lentils and pale flageolet beans, as neither need presoaking or take long to cook; rice (both risotto and long-grain, preferably arborio and basmati), brown and white. Dried fruit: pears, apricots (wild Hunza apricots from Afghanistan, dried with their stones, have by far the best flavour) and prunes, preferably unsulphured and unoiled. No-soak varieties are the most useful.

Flavourings make the most of any fresh ingredients. The ones I would choose are: tomato passata and Whole Earth tomato ketchup; anchovy essence; Worcester sauce; mushroom ketchup; soy sauce; Tabasco; horseradish; mustards (both Dijon and coarse-grain); vinegars (especially balsamic and sherry); elderflower cordial (see p. 106); orange-flower and rose-waters; natural vanilla and almond essences; Earl Grey tea bags (as a base for dried fruit salads, or sorbets and ice-creams); a box of amaretti biscuits, to add, crushed, to ice-creams or crumble toppings; honey (runny more useful than set); whole spices; and a careful selection of dried herbs including fennel stalks, bay leaves, rosemary and oregano. Spices and herbs in particular should be stored in the dark.

SIMONE SEKERS

STARTERS, SNACKS
AND GREEN SALADS

Tarama (smoked cod's roe dip)

Serves 4–6

170g/6oz smoked cod's roe
120ml/4fl. oz olive oil
juice of 1½ lemons

This is the Turkish way of making tarama. Wash the pieces of roe – you do not need to remove the skin as this will lend texture and colour. Put everything in the food processor and blend to a soft cream. Serve with bread or pittas for dipping.

Variation: The Greek version – taramasalata – adds bread soaked in water. Soak 4 large slices of white bread, crusts removed, in water just to cover. Put them in a blender or food processor with their water and 110g/4oz smoked cod's roe. Blend until smooth, then, with the blender or food processor running very slowly, add the juice of 1 or more lemons to taste and up to 150ml/5fl. oz olive oil, enough to get the desired consistency. Taste for sharpness, and finish if you like with a very small, very finely grated onion.

CLAUDIA RODEN

Simone Sekers writes: TARAMA, or salted and smoked cod's roe, has become popular as the basic ingredient for the Greek *mezze* taramasalata, although it is also good eaten on its own, thinly sliced. It can sometimes be rather hard, and will therefore need soaking overnight before making into taramasalata. It will keep in the freezer for a short time.

GREEN salads made with a variety of the many salad plants and fresh herbs now available make quite the best instant first courses and are a wonderful pick-me-up and appetite sharpener. Suitable salad leaves include all the various lettuce varieties, chicories and watercress, plus herbs such as basil, dill, mint, tarragon, sorrel, chervil, chives, coriander, chopped spring onions, celery leaves and tufts of young parsley. Some shops sell rocket and lamb's lettuce, both marvellous additions. If you are a gardener or have gardening friends, grow a little patch of rocket, lamb's lettuce, claytonia, Greek cress and land cress, and use a few edible flowers – nasturtium, heartsease, borage, marigold petals – as a garnish. Washed and dried, they will keep perfectly fresh for a couple of days in a sealed plastic bag in the refrigerator, ready to take out and shake on to the plate.

Almost anything you enjoy can be used to top the salads: strips of fennel and red pepper (either raw, or grilled, skinned, then kept under olive oil), diced tomato and cucumber, chopped walnuts and fried pine nuts, toasted almond flakes, frizzled strips of bacon, tiny croutons, chopped olives, anchovies and capers, chopped hard-boiled eggs, chopped beetroot tossed in a few caraway seeds, tiny cooked broccoli or cauliflower florets, segments of orange, and so on. Choose a selection as you see fit, remembering that the idea is not to have them all, but to provide a few extras to enhance the overall piquancy and flavour. Dress by dribbling over your favourite oil or vinaigrette, or, say, mix the eggs with mayonnaise, the cucumber with sour cream, and the beetroot with yoghurt, piling little blobs in the centre of the salad, and dribbling oil over the leaves.

Salade tiède

Salades tièdes – warm salads – are an excellent way of turning a simple green salad into something more substantial. The idea is to have something hot and tasty on top of the leaves, moistened with some kind of warm dressing or the cooking juices. Any strips of meat, bacon, chicken livers, grilled strips of confit, or leftover chicken or small pieces of fish or shellfish are suitable. Grilled goat's cheese is especially good. So are slices of leftover sausage (if a decent kind), served with an onion marmalade or your favourite chutney, chopped to a sauce-like consistency. The following is one more idea to try. For another, see the scallop and broad bean salad on p. 63.

LYNDA BROWN

Hot kidney salad with ginger and Marsala

Allow 1 fresh lamb's kidney per person. Halve, remove the tubes and slice thickly. Toss in a little butter in a non-stick pan over a high heat for 30–60 seconds. For 4 people, add 1 teaspoon of finely chopped preserved ginger, and 90–120ml/3–4fl. oz Marsala. Cook vigorously for 1–2 minutes. (Don't overcook the kidneys. As soon as red juices start to ooze out, they are ready.) Take out, boiling down the sauce a little longer if necessary. Spoon the kidneys and sauce over the waiting salad leaves. Finish with an optional dribble of cream and serve immediately.

LYNDA BROWN

Lemon and chervil soup

This is a great standby soup with a lovely fresh lemon flavour.

Serves 4

600ml/1pt fine-flavoured fish stock
1 tbsp rice
juice of 1 large lemon, beaten with 2 eggs
1 tbsp chervil, finely chopped

Simmer the rice in the fish stock in a covered pan until tender, about 5–10 minutes. Have the lemon and egg mixture ready in a bowl. Add a ladleful of stock, whisk together, then tip the mixture into the rest of the stock in the pan. Keep whisking and cook until the mixture is very hot and thickens slightly – on no account let it boil, or it will curdle. Stir in the chervil and serve immediately, in hot soup bowls.

LYNDA BROWN

French beans with sesame seeds ⓥ

Serves 4

340g/12oz young French beans, topped and tailed
1–2 tbsp light sesame seed oil
3 tsp sesame seeds

Blanch the beans in boiling water for 2–3 minutes. Drain, then toss in the sesame seed oil while still warm. Toast the sesame seeds until light brown, then pound briefly with a pinch of salt in a pestle and mortar to release their aroma. Lightly mix half into the beans, arrange the beans in a dish or on separate plates, and scatter the rest of the sesame seeds on top.

LYNDA BROWN

Yan-kit So's stir-fried mange-touts ⓥ

This recipe comes from the well-known Chinese cookery author, Yan-kit So, which Claudia Roden included in one of her articles.

Serves 4

340g/12oz mange-touts, rinsed, topped and tailed
2 tbsp vegetable oil for frying
1 bunch spring onions, trimmed and cut into 5cm/2in
lengths, white and green parts separated
3 tbsp well-seasoned ham or chicken stock
salt to taste

Heat a wok (or use a large sauté or non-stick frying pan) over a high heat until hot. Add the oil and swirl around. Add the white spring onions, stir for a few seconds to release their aroma, then add the mange-touts, turning and stir-frying for a few seconds before reducing the heat to medium so as not to burn them. Add the stock, cover and continue to cook for about 2 minutes, at the end of which the mange-touts should be cooked yet crisp. Season to taste and mix in the green spring onion. Serve immediately.

Sweetcorn, ginger and pepper stir-fry ⓥ

Serves 4

2 large corn on the cob, cooked (approx. 225g/8oz
stripped weight; or use 225g/8oz tinned or defrosted
corn)
1–2 tbsp vegetable oil
1 dsp finely grated fresh ginger
2 tsp preserved ginger, finely chopped
1 fresh green chilli, de-seeded and finely chopped
2 green peppers, de-seeded and cut into very thin strips
2 spring onions, green and white part, finely chopped
(optional)
few drops chilli/Tabasco/hot pepper sauce, or
soy sauce

Strip the corn from the cobs and set aside. Heat the oil in a non-stick frying pan, add both kinds of ginger and the chilli and sizzle for 30 seconds. Add the peppers and stir-fry for 2 minutes over a high heat. Add the sweetcorn and toss to heat through. Pile on to a serving dish, mix in the spring onions if using, sprinkle lightly with your chosen sauce (be sparing with the hot variety) and serve immediately. Cooked prawns can also be added. Add them with the sweetcorn and let them heat through.

LYNDA BROWN

Tinned beans

Tinned beans – kidney, haricot, butter beans and chick peas – are a godsend when you are busy, hard up, or have hungry people to feed. With a few extra embellishments they can be served hot as a meal in themselves, with bread to soak up the sauce, or cold in salads. Here are some suggestions from Claudia Roden and Thane Prince.

With bacon: Fry small pieces of bacon in a pan until they brown. Add 2 cloves of crushed garlic and, before this colours, add a large tin of beans (340g/12oz) with their juice. Season with salt, pepper, cinnamon, ground cloves and mace. Cook gently until the flavours have been absorbed.

CLAUDIA RODEN

With sage and tomato: Cook the beans with chopped peeled tomatoes and a sprig of sage, seasoning with salt and pepper until the flavours are absorbed.

CLAUDIA RODEN

Bean salad. Mix together 340g/12oz each of drained red kidney beans and chick peas or white beans, 2 coarsely grated medium carrots, 1 chopped red onion, 1 tbsp of chervil, parsley, chives or any chopped fresh herb, and 4–6 tbsp of your favourite French dressing.

THANE PRINCE

Vegetable pot ⓥ

All kinds of vegetables can be used for this dish: Brussels sprouts, courgettes (left whole if tiny), cauliflower or broccoli cut into florets, a few fresh peas or broad beans, mange-touts, thin slices of pumpkin and turnips and tomatoes with their skins removed, even lettuce hearts and radicchio cut in half. Use as many different vegetables as possible.

Put them in a pan with a tight-fitting lid so that they will steam in their own juices. Sprinkle with salt and pepper and 1–2 tbsp of oil. Add a bunch of chopped herbs such as parsley, basil, chervil, tarragon or mint, spring onion, and, if you like, a squeeze of lemon. Moisten with about

159

90–120ml/3–4fl. oz water, put the lid on and cook for 6–10 minutes, or until the vegetables are done.

CLAUDIA RODEN

Bread and cheese omelette ⓥ

Serves 1

1 slice good bread, crusts removed and cut into cubes
approx. 30g/1oz butter, plus 2 tbsp oil for frying
2 eggs
salt and pepper
1 tbsp grated Gruyère or Cheddar cheese

Fry the cubes of bread in a mixture of the butter and oil until very crisp and brown. Drain these croutons on kitchen paper and set aside. Make the omelette in the usual way and, when it is just set underneath and still soft in the middle, season, add the croutons and the cheese. Fold over and serve at once.

SIMONE SEKERS

Apple omelette dessert

Serves 2

2 large cooking or dessert apples, peeled, cored and
quartered
2–3 tbsp sugar, or to taste
2 tbsp rum, Calvados or a sweet liqueur
1–2 tbsp double cream (optional)
2 large eggs
1 tsp butter

Put the apples in a pan with 1–2 tbsp of sugar and water, cover and let them steam in their own juice for about 10 minutes until they fall apart. Mash them and turn up the heat to dry them out if they are too watery. Add the spirit or liqueur and stir in the cream if using.

Make two small omelettes or one large one: beat the eggs with 1 tbsp sugar, heat the butter in a frying pan, preferably non-stick, and when it sizzles drop in the egg mixture. When the eggs begin to set at the bottom turn the omelette over with the help of a plate. Cook for another minute or so. Serve with the hot apple sauce spread on top.

CLAUDIA RODEN

PASTA

Nothing is nicer, or faster, than pasta in all its various forms. Nor can you ever have enough pasta recipes – here are a few more, traditional and new.

Pesto

Pesto is the ultimate sauce for pasta. Bought jars of pesto are an expensive imitation of the real thing, which takes but a minute to make in a food processor and which, minus the garlic, freezes extremely well. It is important to use fresh garlic, and freshly grated, not packet, Parmesan. If you cannot find decent Parmesan, Sardo pecorino (*see* p. 197), which is milder and creamier (and the cheese I use myself for pesto), is a better choice.

Serves 3–4

55g/2oz fresh basil leaves
30g/1oz pine nuts
1 fat, juicy clove garlic, crushed
30g/1oz freshly grated Parmesan or pecorino cheese
3–4 tbsp cold-pressed fruity olive oil, preferably Tuscan

Put the basil leaves in the food processor and process for a few seconds until chopped. Add the pine nuts and garlic and process again. Add the cheese and, with the motor running, pour in enough olive oil to form a smooth, creamy paste. Serve in a small bowl for people to help themselves.

If you are making pesto to freeze, omit the garlic, adding it later when you come to use the pesto. Chop it finely, to a paste, and incorporate it well.

LYNDA BROWN

Spaghetti carbonara

Ideally, suggests Simone Sekers, you should use fresh tagliatelli for this: 'Alternatively, use good-quality dried pasta, and really good bacon and eggs – wet supermarket bacon simply won't do, and the flavour of genuine free-range eggs makes this a gourmet dish.' See the mail-order list (p. 216) for a good bacon supplier.

Serves 3–4

340g/12oz spaghetti or tagliatelli
225g/8oz bacon
1 tbsp olive oil if necessary (*see* method)
3 large eggs, beaten
salt and pepper
freshly grated Parmesan cheese to serve (*see* p. 197)

Warm a serving bowl in the oven. Cook the pasta in boiling water until *al dente*. Meanwhile, cut the bacon into strips and fry it until crisp. If the bacon is too lean or too wet, add a generous spoonful of olive oil to the pan to help it out. Drain the pasta, transfer it to the warmed bowl and quickly mix the eggs well into the pasta. The heat will cook the eggs lightly to form a sauce. Add salt and pepper and the bacon and its fat and serve at once on very hot plates with freshly grated Parmesan.

SIMONE SEKERS

Editor's note: This is one of the best pasta dishes but needs a little care to get right. It is important not to scramble the eggs – they should just cook sufficiently to thicken and form a sauce, hence the hot bowl and very hot pasta to start with. Wholewheat pasta is also good for this dish.

Pasta with Gorgonzola sauce Ⓥ

Serves 2

225g/8oz spaghetti or short pasta
100g/3½ oz Gorgonzola cheese
90ml/3fl. oz milk
pepper
a grating of nutmeg (optional)

Cook the pasta until *al dente* by throwing it into rapidly boiling salted water. Stir to prevent it sticking, and begin to taste for 'doneness' when it starts to swell and rise to the surface.

For the sauce, crush the Gorgonzola with a fork in a small pan, heat gently, add the milk, and blend well, then season with pepper and nutmeg, if using, to taste (the Gorgonzola will be sufficiently salty). Drain the pasta quickly, mix with the sauce and serve at once on hot plates.

CLAUDIA RODEN

Pasta with frizzled parsley and anchovy sauce

Serves 2

225g/8oz pasta
4–5 tbsp fruity olive oil
2 dried chillis
1 fat clove garlic, finely chopped
2 tbsp chopped parsley
2 anchovy fillets, chopped
toasted or fried breadcrumbs for sprinkling (optional)

Cook the pasta in the usual way and have hot plates or pasta bowls ready. Meanwhile, heat 1 tbsp olive oil with the chillis in a very small pan (I have a small, deep-sided pan, about the size and depth of a dariole mould, for melting butter which is ideal for this and similar sauces). Add the garlic and cook for 30 seconds or so to release its aroma. Add the parsley and cook for another minute or so. Off the heat stir in the anchovies until they dissolve into the sauce. Stir in the extra oil. Either toss the pasta in the sauce or put the sauce on the table for people to spoon over themselves. Do not eat the chillis and warn people likewise. Toasted or fried breadcrumbs – both of which are extraordinarily good with pasta – can be added, put in a bowl and offered separately, to be sprinkled over at the table.

LYNDA BROWN

Fresh pasta with sour cream, mushrooms and tarragon ✓

Serves 4

450g/1lb fresh pasta
170g/6oz button mushrooms, finely sliced
30g/1oz butter
1 tbsp dry sherry
300ml/10fl. oz sour cream
1–2 tbsp chopped fresh tarragon, or 1 tbsp dried
salt and pepper
freshly grated Parmesan cheese (*see* p. 197)

Cook the pasta in plenty of boiling water until *al dente*. Fry the mushrooms for 4–5 minutes in the butter over a high heat. Add the sherry and continue to cook until most of the liquid has evaporated. Lower the heat, stir in the sour cream and warm through. It must not boil. Add the tarragon, salt and plenty of freshly ground black pepper. Toss the drained pasta with the sauce, and sprinkle with freshly grated Parmesan. Serve with a side salad and *ciabatta* bread.

THANE PRINCE

See also: Pasta with olive and mushroom sauce, p. 102.

RICE

When it comes to fast cooking, rice is as valuable as pasta, either to accompany grilled or pan-fried meat and fish, or as the base for an impromptu pilaf or stir-fry. Leftover rice can be fried, turned into salads or added to soups. It can be spiced in any number of ways, chopped herbs can be added for extra fragrance, or a pat of savoury butter stirred in just before serving.

My own method of cooking rice is unconventional, and very quick. It produces a very nutty rice, each grain separate, and will keep perfectly for up to half an hour on a warming tray. If you prefer a softer rice, add a little extra water. Basmati rice has by far the best flavour and is the one I use for this method.

Quick-cook rice (√)

Put the rice (no need to wash) in a heavy pan with a tight-fitting lid. Add water barely to cover and season lightly with salt. Cover tightly, bring to the boil and boil hard for 1 minute. Turn off the heat and let the rice stand for 5–10 minutes; the rice will continue to cook in its own steam. Uncover and stir with a fork to loosen and redistribute the grains. Serve or keep warm until required.

LYNDA BROWN

Quick-cook brown rice (√)

Brown rice can also be cooked quickly. This time cover the rice with about 5cm/2in of water. Cover and cook steadily for 5 minutes. Turn off the heat and let the rice sit for about 10–15 minutes. Again the rice continues to cook in the residual heat. Drain off the water (it is often dirty and may have some scum) and test the rice: it should be almost soft. Add fresh water to cover and continue to cook gently, covered, for another 5 minutes or so until soft but still chewy.

LYNDA BROWN

Savoury rice or Chinese noodles

Variations of this dish – rice or Chinese noodles topped with a tasty stir-fry topping – have provided inspiration for many mid-week suppers over the years. Ingredients and seasonings can be varied to suit. I have suggested soy sauce as a seasoning, but hoi-sin sauce diluted with a little water, oyster sauce or a few drops of sesame seed oil can be used with equal success. Other good vegetables to add include broccoli, mushrooms, a little grated carrot and a chopped tomato or two. The omelette strips can be left out but turn the dish into more of a meal and are very tasty.

Serves 3–4

340g/12oz cooked hot rice, or Chinese noodles

For the Chinese omelettes (optional)
2 eggs, beaten with 1 tbsp sesame seeds
vegetable oil for greasing
1–2 tbsp sherry

For the topping
1 small onion/few spring onions/1 leek, finely chopped
1–2 tbsp vegetable oil
1/2 red or green pepper, diced
110g/4oz cooked peas or sweetcorn
110–170g/4–6oz prawns/chicken meat/ham/lightly
cooked chicken liver/strips of tender beef or lamb
soy sauce

First make the omelettes, if using. Heat a lightly greased omelette pan. Using just enough mixture to coat the base of the pan thinly, make 4–5 thin omelettes as you would pancakes. When one side is cooked, turn the omelette over and cook the other side for about 1 minute. Lift one edge of the omelette and pour in 1 tsp sherry – it will sizzle violently. Remove, roll up and set aside. Make all the omelettes in the same way. Cut into strips and keep warm.

Soften the onion/spring onion/leek in 1 tbsp oil in a non-stick frying pan. Add the peppers and any other uncooked vegetables of your choice and continue cooking until soft or done to your liking, followed by the peas and meat or prawns. Heat through thoroughly, then spoon the mixture over the top of the rice. Decorate with the strips of omelette, sprinkle with a few drops of soy or other sauce and serve immediately.

LYNDA BROWN

Spiced rice pilaf (√)

Serves 4

285g/10oz long-grain rice
1/2 tsp cumin seeds
1/2 tsp coriander seeds
4 cardamom pods
5cm/2in cinnamon stick
1 tbsp oil or butter
1 small onion, finely chopped
1/2 tsp turmeric
750ml/1¼ pt water
1/4 tsp salt
freshly ground black pepper
toasted nuts (optional)

Put the whole spices and seeds from the cardamom pods into a mortar and crush lightly with a pestle. Heat the oil or butter in a largish pan and fry the onion until transparent. Add the crushed spices and turmeric and stir-fry for 1 minute. Put in the rice, water, salt and a few turns of black pepper, bring to the boil and simmer over a low heat until the rice is cooked and the liquid absorbed, about 20 minutes. A few toasted nuts can be sprinkled on top. Serve with grilled chicken and salad, or a vegetable curry and cucumber raita.

THANE PRINCE

MEAT DISHES

Lamb chops with date sauce

Serves 2

2 lamb chops
1½ tbsp light vegetable oil
⅔ tsp cinnamon
¼ tsp allspice
salt and pepper
6–8 dried dates, pitted

Mix together the oil, cinnamon, allspice, salt and pepper, and turn the chops in the mixture. Put them under the grill and cook them, turning once, until they are nicely browned outside but still pink and juicy inside.

For the sauce, which can be cooked while the chops are grilling, cover the dates with water and simmer until they are soft enough to mash with a fork – it takes minutes only – adding extra water if necessary. The mixture should be creamy. Serve the sauce over or under the chops.

CLAUDIA RODEN

Best-ever hamburgers

This is one of Thane Prince's best-known and best-loved recipes.

Serves 4

450g/1lb good-quality beef mince
2 tbsp double cream
½ red onion
1 fat clove garlic
1–2 tbsp chopped parsley
salt and pepper
oil for brushing

If you have a food processor, assembling these hamburgers will take only a few seconds. Put the cream, onion, garlic and parsley in the bowl, season well and process until the onion is chopped. Add the mince and give the mixture a few quick bursts to combine everything – don't leave the machine running for more than a few seconds or you will get meat paste.

Otherwise, chop the onion and garlic by hand and mix everything together in a large bowl.

Divide the mixture into 4 portions and shape each one by hand into a round patty about 3.75cm/½ in deep. Heat a griddle or heavy frying pan and, if necessary, brush very lightly with oil (the hamburgers will give off their own fat). Cook them for about 5 minutes on each side. Serve in a toasted muffin with thick slices of mild onion, beef tomato and iceberg lettuce.

Variation: Substitute lamb, yoghurt and mint for the beef, cream and parsley.

THANE PRINCE

Sweet and sour Venetian liver

You won't find a faster or better recipe than this simple, nutritious dish from Claudia Roden, which can just as easily be made for one or two people. I prefer to use a non-stick pan. Don't be afraid, either, to cook the liver for less time (a minute either side) if you wish, letting it rest in a warm place while you eat the first course.

Serves 4

2 tbsp butter
1 tbsp sunflower or olive oil
450g/1lb calves' liver, thinly sliced
salt and pepper
1 tsp sugar, or more to taste
juice of ½ –1 lemon

Heat the butter and oil in a frying pan until sizzling, and fry the liver for 4 minutes over a high heat. Add salt and pepper, and turn the slices over once. Push the liver to the side of the pan to leave room for making the sauce. Lower the heat, add the lemon and then the sugar to the other side of the pan and blend quickly to dissolve the sugar. Mix with the liver and cook for a few seconds more so that the liver is done but still pink inside. Serve at once with rice or pasta.

Note: As lemons vary so much in size and sharpness it is important to start with a little lemon juice and add more to taste, and then decide for yourself just how much sugar is needed.

CLAUDIA RODEN

FRESH FRUIT SALADS
AND SIMPLE DESSERTS

It is one of the great mysteries of life that, although apples, oranges and other fruits are perfectly enjoyable on their own, chopped up and turned into a fruit salad they become colourful, refreshing and eminently more desirable. Here are three suggestions from Simone Sekers. As she stresses, improvisation is the thing here, so use the quantities and flavourings as a guide, making the fruit salad as you wish: 'In all three salads – and other fruit salads – only add sugar to taste (icing sugar dissolves best), not as a reflex action. If adding alcohol, go for fruit *eaux de vie* rather than sticky liqueurs, Cointreau being the exception.'

Pineapple, mango and blackberry fruit salad

Serves 4

340g/12oz tinned pineapple pieces in natural juice
1 pawpaw, peeled and seeds removed
2 ripe mangoes, peeled and sliced
225g/8oz frozen blackberries
300ml/10fl. oz carton freshly squeezed orange juice
2 tsp rose-water

Mix everything together and serve as soon as the blackberries have defrosted; they will chill the rest of the ingredients.

Peach, berry and elderflower cordial salad

Serves 4

340g/12oz tinned white sliced peaches in natural juice
450g/1lb packet frozen berries (usually raspberries and blackcurrants), available from supermarket freezer cabinets
elderflower cordial, diluted with mineral water to taste

Mix as before.

Apricot, mandarin orange, pear and Earl Grey salad

Serves 4

340g/12oz tinned apricots in natural juice
1 300ml/10fl. oz tinned mandarin oranges in natural
juice
2 fresh, ripe Comice pears, sliced
300ml/10fl. oz Earl Grey tea, made with a teabag

Make a medium-strong infusion of Earl Grey tea (remove the teabag before it becomes too bitter) and mix as before.   SIMONE SEKERS

Pears with almonds or hazelnuts

This is my favourite instant dessert. Choose ripe juicy pears, preferably Comice, William or Beurre Hardy. Allow 1 pear per person. Peel, core, halve and slice each half into four. Arrange in individual shallow dishes and pour 1–2 tbsp of Poire William over each portion. Scatter with either toasted almond flakes or whole toasted almonds cut into strips, or toasted hazelnuts, rubbed to remove their skins and chopped coarsely.

LYNDA BROWN

Heiss Himbeer

Hot raspberries make an instant, healthy and delicious dessert. This recipe is especially useful in winter for using up frozen raspberries. Heat the raspberries in a pan with sugar to taste for 2–3 minutes until thoroughly hot but not completely disintegrated, and serve in fruit dishes. A couple of tablespoons of *crème de Cassis* is an excellent addition. If using frozen raspberries, allow a little longer cooking and use a gentle heat.

LYNDA BROWN

Apricots with almond paste

This is an idea I have adapted from one of Claudia Roden's recipes. Allow 2 ripe apricots per person. Slice them in half, remove the stone, and arrange in a single layer in an ovenproof dish. Mix an equal quantity of ground almonds and caster sugar to a paste with a little rose- or orange-flower water (1 tbsp of each plus 1 tsp of flower essence is sufficient for 4 halves). Fill the cavities with the paste and put under the grill for 5 minutes or so until the apricots are hot and the filling has formed a light brown crust. Ripe peaches can be treated in the same way.

LYNDA BROWN

Bananas and cream

Serves 4

Slice 4 medium ripe bananas. Whip 150ml/5fl. oz of double or whipping cream until almost stiff, fold in 150ml/5fl. oz plain yoghurt or sour cream and spread over the bananas. Toast 3–4 tbsp slivered almonds or almond flakes in a dry frying pan and sprinkle over the bananas, together with 1–2 tbsp muscovado sugar. Flavour the cream, if you like, with cinnamon, grated orange rind or rum.

THANE PRINCE

Zabaglione

There is no finer end to an impromptu meal than this light and comforting foamy mass of egg yolks and Marsala which reaches the parts all other desserts miss. At home, I make it so frequently that it could probably make itself. This is Claudia Roden's recipe.

Serves 6

8 large egg yolks
85–110g/3–4oz sugar
240ml/8fl. oz Marsala

Beat the egg yolks with the sugar until pale, then beat in the Marsala. Pour into a large saucepan and heat gently by standing the pan in a larger pan of barely simmering water. Beat constantly – an electric beater is a help – until the mixture swells to a thick foam. Pile into warm glasses and serve immediately.

CLAUDIA RODEN

Editor's note: Zabaglione can be easily made for one or two. As a general guide, allow 1 egg yolk, 15g/½ oz sugar and 30–60ml/1–2fl. oz Marsala per person. Put everything in a large bowl set over a pan of simmering water. Using an electric whisk, whisk until light and foamy, about 5 minutes or so, adding a little extra sugar or Marsala to taste. If you prefer a thicker, less foamy zabaglione, whisk by hand using a balloon whisk.

The French and
Italian Connection

I KNOW OF no cook, myself included, who does not have a special affection for the food of France, or who does not delight in experiencing all its tastes and smells at first hand. The same may be said about Italy. As Claudia Roden – an expert on Italian cuisine – has remarked, it is easy to fall under the spell of Italy. Having started with pizza and pasta, and fallen in love with olive oil, we are now discovering the many and varied regional aspects of Italian food and learning to appreciate its simple charms, rustic tastes, vibrant flavours and wide diversity.

For this section, I have chosen dishes which offer a glimpse of French and Italian cooking and which can be re-created with confidence at home. Many are admirably suited to eating out of doors, or for the kind of informal entertaining we increasingly prefer today. Most of the recipes have been collected abroad, while others are based firmly in the French and Italian tradition. A few other recipes – for fish, for example – will be found elsewhere in the book.

OLIVE OIL

The great French chef Auguste Escoffier was accused of the 'butterisation' of his native Provence, eschewing the traditional olive oil in favour of more refined lubrication. We have witnessed the opposite in this country over the past 10 years, and the 'olivisation' of Britain has meant that every supermarket offers at least three varieties, usually extra-virgin, virgin, and just olive oil. The latter lacks much of the flavour of the first two, but is more generally useful, for frying and browning meat for stews, and for making such things as mayonnaise, where the pungency of extra-virgin can obliterate more delicate flavours. The flavour of extra-virgin oil is to be savoured on pasta, baked potatoes, and on robust salads such as those made from lentils, beans or potatoes.

Extra-virgin and virgin oils are the most expensive, ranging from £3–4 for a litre bottle for a supermarket own brand, which can often be very good indeed, to £15–20 for the 'single malts' of the olive oil world, from named estates in Tuscany and Provence, where the olives are grown organically. What you spend depends very much on your own palate; I know several excellent cooks who find the sharp peppery quality of a young 'first cold pressing' oil from Tuscany far too aggressive, while others revel in the thick, fruity, green oils of Greece. My own current favourite is that produced by Henri Bellon at the Moulin de Badarrides, Fontvielle, in Provence, which we buy when we are passing. As this isn't enough to keep us supplied all year round, I fall back on Waitrose's own-brand extra-virgin oil, and a lovely light oil from the Vaucluse bottled by Taylor and Lake.

Olive oil is no more fattening than any other oil – all oils contain the same number of calories – and olive oil is more generously endowed than other oils with the mono-saturates that are good for you.

SIMONE SEKERS

Editor's note: Extra-virgin and virgin olive oils are produced from the first (cold) pressing of the olives, which is what makes them the most expensive, the difference between them relating to the relative acidity due to the presence of oleic acid. The lesser the acidity, the finer, in general terms, is the olive oil. Extra-virgin oil has an acidity of less than 1 per cent, virgin oils 1–3 per cent. Pure olive oil is actually something of a misnomer, and is produced by highly refining the residue remaining after the initial pressing of the olives, to which is added back a proportion of extra-virgin oil to give it flavour.

FRANCE

VEGETABLE DISHES AND STARTERS

Leeks vinaigrette (√)

Serves 4

8 small leeks
1 tbsp or more wine vinegar
6 tbsp olive oil
small bunch of parsley, finely chopped
salt and pepper

Trim the leeks, slit down one side and wash any earth from between the leaves. Boil the whole leeks in salted water for about 7–10 minutes or until tender, drain well, pour over the rest of the ingredients well beaten together, and serve either warm or cold.

CLAUDIA RODEN

Editor's note: Though extremely simple, this popular French dish is one of the best ways to serve leeks. They look most attractive arranged in a single layer on a white plate with the dressing spooned over. A mustard vinaigrette also goes beautifully with this dish

Marinated vegetables 'à la Grecque' ✓

Serves 4–6

225g/8oz cleaned leeks cut into 1in slices
225g/8oz bulb fennel, cut into eighths
225g/8oz button mushrooms, wiped
110g/4oz celery, sliced
4 tbsp olive oil
300ml/10fl. oz dry white wine
55g/2oz sun-dried tomatoes cut into strips (*see* p. 30)
3–4 plump cloves garlic, crushed
1 tsp each coriander seeds and dried thyme
1/2 tsp black peppercorns
2 bay leaves
salt to taste
1 tbsp balsamic vinegar (optional) (*see* p. 65)

Toss the prepared vegetables in the heated oil in a large pan. They should be well covered with the oil and starting to cook. Add all the remaining ingredients except the balsamic vinegar and, if the wine does not cover the vegetables, a little water.

Bring to the boil and simmer for up to 10 minutes, depending on how crisp you like your vegetables. Remove the vegetables from the pan and boil rapidly to reduce by a third. Remove from the heat and pour over the reserved vegetables. Add the vinegar if using. Allow the vegetables to marinate in the refrigerator for at least 24 hours. Remove 1 hour before serving. Serve with crusty bread.

THANE PRINCE

See also: Olive and olivade anchovy paste, p. 117.

Blanched garlic and sorrel soup ⓥ

Along with the rest of south-western France, the cooking of the Dordogne has become one of the most popular of France's regional cuisines over the last few years. One of the dishes I enjoyed most when I visited the area was the local version of the thick traditional onion and garlic soup known as *tourin*, made with the addition of handfuls of tender young sorrel. It is surprisingly mild and restorative, and is one of the best summer soups to make when fresh garlic comes into the shops, if you can lay your hands on sorrel, or have it growing in the garden.

Serves 6

100g/3½ oz fresh garlic cloves, peeled
generous 500g/1lb onions, finely sliced and chopped
2 tbsp vegetable oil, or oil and butter mixed
1 tbsp flour
1l /1¾ pt water

To finish
170g/6oz sorrel, stalks removed
2 eggs, separated
salt and pepper

Put the garlic in a small pan, cover with water, and bring to the boil. Drain. Repeat the blanching twice more, using fresh water each time, then slice the garlic cloves finely. Gently soften the onion and garlic in the vegetable oil/butter in a covered pan for 15–20 minutes, stirring frequently. Stir in the flour, season lightly, add the water and simmer for 45 minutes. At this point you can cool the soup and reheat it later.

Cook the sorrel in a separate pan over a gentle heat (you will not need to add any water) until wilted, 2–3 minutes. Bring the soup to the boil and add the sorrel. Lightly break up the egg whites with a fork and stir into the soup, stirring round to form thin threads. Off the heat, beat in the egg yolks. Serve immediately in hot soup plates, and, if you like, follow the local custom and *faire chabrol* – swill the last few spoonfuls of soup with a little wine and drink.

LYNDA BROWN

THE following two recipes, again from Claudia Roden, are redolent with garlic and sun-drenched herbs, and come from Provence. Try to use fresh garlic if you can; in any event avoid any which is stale or rancid.

Daube d'aubergines Ⓥ

Serves 6

675g/1½ lb aubergines
675g/1½ lb ripe tomatoes, peeled and chopped
½ bottle red wine
2–3 tsp sugar
1 garlic clove, crushed
1 tsp dried thyme
1 bay leaf
salt and pepper
sunflower or olive oil for frying
small bunch parsley, chopped

Peel the aubergines, cut them in half lengthways and then into thick slices. Sprinkle with salt and leave to drain in a colander for 30 minutes. Meanwhile, place the tomatoes, wine, sugar, garlic, thyme, bay leaf, and a very little salt and pepper in a large pot and simmer over a low heat for about 20 minutes.

Rinse the salt off the aubergines, dry them with a cloth and shallow-fry in hot oil. Turn them over once to brown them all over, then remove with a slotted spoon and squeeze gently on kitchen paper. Add the aubergines to the tomato sauce and simmer very gently, covered, adding a little water if necessary, for about 30 minutes. Add the parsley towards the end of cooking. It is as good cold as it is hot.

CLAUDIA RODEN

Tian of courgettes Ⓥ

Serves 8–10

1.5kg/3lb courgettes
2 large onions, chopped
1 garlic clove, finely chopped
3 tbsp olive oil
225g/8oz short-grain rice
3 eggs
8–10 Swiss chard leaves or 110g/4oz spinach, shredded
large bunch parsley, finely chopped
small bunch basil, finely chopped
55g/2oz Parmesan, grated (*see* p. 197)
salt and pepper

Trim the courgettes but leave them whole and unpeeled. Boil in salted water for about 20 minutes, or steam until tender. Mash with a potato masher in a colander and let the juices drain away. Fry the onions and garlic in 2 tbsp of the olive oil till golden. Cook the rice in boiling salted water for 10 minutes or until it is still not quite done, then drain.

Preheat the oven to 200°C/400°F/gas mark 6. Beat the eggs lightly in a bowl. Mix in the Swiss chard or spinach, add the parsley and basil, the Parmesan and pepper, and then the mashed courgettes, fried onion and garlic and rice. Mix well and taste before adding salt before the Parmesan is salty.

Oil a large earthenware dish with the remaining 1 tbsp of oil and pour the mixture in. Bake for about 40 minutes or until firm and browned on top. Serve hot.

CLAUDIA RODEN

Editor's note: A *tian* is a shallow oval vegetable baking dish. It has become especially associated with this dish, in which the vegetable is baked with eggs and rice to form a cake which can be sliced into wedges. Spinach and Swiss chard also make excellent *tians*.

Pissaladière

I will never forget my first taste of pissaladière, the famous onion and anchovy tart of Nice. It is every bit as good as pizza, and even more savoury. The slow, patient cooking of the onions is what makes the tart, for they break down into a mellow and sweet creamy mass, quite distinct and much more delicious, so I discovered, than ordinary fried onions. In Nice, Claudia Roden writes, the layer of onion is as thick as the layer of bread and is cooked almost to a purée and never allowed to brown. To make life easier, use a food processor to slice the onions. This is Claudia Roden's recipe.

Serves 6

For the dough
225g/8oz plain flour
1 egg, beaten
3/4 tsp salt
15g/1/2oz fresh yeast, or 1½ tsp dried yeast
1/4 tsp sugar
90ml/3fl. oz warm water
few drops of olive oil

For the filling
1.125kg/2½ lb onions, thinly sliced
3–4 tbsp olive oil, plus extra for greasing
2 tsp mixed chopped fresh herbs such as basil, thyme
and rosemary
salt and pepper
12 or more anchovy fillets, cut into halves
a few black olives, stoned and halved (*see* p. 117)

To make the bread dough, sift the flour into a bowl and make a well in the centre. Put the beaten egg and salt into the well. Put the yeast, sugar and water into a small bowl and leave until frothy. Gradually stir the yeast mixture into the flour, mixing it with your fingers to form a ball of soft dough. Add a little flour if it is too sticky and knead well with your hands for 10 minutes or until the dough is smooth and elastic. Pour a drop or two of olive oil on the dough and turn it in your hands so that it becomes lightly oiled all over. Cover with a damp cloth and leave to rise in a warm place for an hour or until doubled in bulk.

While the dough is rising, make the filling. Cook the onions in the olive oil in a covered pan on a very low flame, stirring occasionally, for 40 minutes or until they are very soft. Add the herbs, salt and pepper and continue to cook for a few minutes longer. Preheat the oven to 190°C/375°F/gas mark 5. Grease a pie plate or flan dish about 35cm/14in in diameter with oil. Punch the dough down, knead it lightly and press it into the pie pan with the palms of your hands. Spread the onion mixture over the dough and make a lattice pattern of anchovy fillets on top. Put half an olive in the middle of each square. Let the dough rise again for 10–15 minutes, then bake for 25–30 minutes or until the bread base is cooked. Serve hot.

CLAUDIA RODEN

Piperade Ⓥ

Piperade, a creamy mixture of eggs, tomatoes and sweet peppers, is the national dish of Pays Basque, the fiercely independent rural backwater of rolling countryside and small neat villages located deep in the corner of south-western France which borders Spain.

This version comes from Monsieur Arcé, chef/proprietor of Hotel Arcé in St Etienne de Baigorry, which has held a Michelin rosette for its cooking for longer than anywhere else in France. He uses the local long thin green variety of pepper called *espelette*, but the kind of pepper we get here is just as suitable. Often, piperade is made like scrambled eggs, but Monsieur Arcé prefers to make his like an omelette. Serve on its own or with ham, bacon or spicy continental type sausages. Sauce Basquaise, the basis of piperade, is ubiquitous in the region, and can be used with chicken (see below) or fish, or other vegetables. It freezes well, and is well worth making in quantity in late summer when tomatoes and peppers are ripe and plentiful.

Serves 4

For the sauce Basquaise
2 large green peppers, de-seeded and coarsely chopped
1 large onion, chopped fairly finely
1–2 tbsp vegetable oil, or duck or goose fat
450–560g/1¼lb very ripe tomatoes, skinned and
coarsely chopped
salt and pepper

6–7 eggs, lightly beaten

To make the sauce Basquaise, soften the peppers and onion in the oil over a gentle heat for about 15 minutes. Add the tomatoes and cook steadily for another 15–20 minutes. Season if necessary and set aside. This quantity makes about 600ml/1pt of sauce.

Unless you have a really large frying pan, divide the eggs and the sauce in half and make two separate piperades. Reheat the sauce, draining off the excess liquid (the sauce should be chunky and not watery; save the liquid for soups). Add the hot sauce to the eggs, mix well and tip into a hot frying pan, preferably non-stick, lubricated with a little oil. Make an omelette in the usual way, keeping it runny in the centre. Fold, divide into two and serve on hot plates. Accompany with salad and bread.

LYNDA BROWN

Poulet Basquaise

This excellent summer dish, found all over Pays Basque, is easily adapted to the number of people needing to be fed. Brown jointed chicken pieces evenly in their own fat over a gentle heat until almost cooked through, turning them frequently. Give them a good 20–25 minutes. Drain off the fat. For four people, add about 600ml/1pt of sauce Basquaise. Turn the chicken pieces in the sauce, cover, and cook until tender. Serve with rice and salad.

LYNDA BROWN

MEAT DISHES

Farçon savoyard

The following recipe, from the charming Auberge du Bois Prin in Chamonix in the Savoie region of France, is a real collector's piece. A traditional (and unlikely-sounding combination until you have tried it) dish of potatoes and dried fruit, eaten on Sundays after church with a glass of local wine and salad, it makes an excellent accompaniment to pork or any kind of game, which is the modern way of serving it.

It is traditionally made in a straight-sided *kugelhupf* mould, but an oblong terrine or loaf tin will suffice. It is important to cover the container tightly, otherwise the terrine can become over-brown during the lengthy cooking time.

Serves 6

approx. 110–170g/4–6oz thinly sliced good-quality
streaky bacon, smoked or unsmoked
500g/generous 1lb potatoes, peeled
1 egg, beaten
1 tbsp flour
4 tbsp cream
10 large pitted prunes
5 dried pear halves, sliced in half

Line your container with bacon. Grate the potatoes finely – I use the grating attachment on my food processor. Mix thoroughly with the rest of the ingredients, adding the dried fruit last, and pile into the container; Ideally you want a depth of about 7.5cm/3in. Cover *very* tightly with aluminium foil (a sheet of greaseproof paper inserted between the foil and container is a good idea). Place in a roasting tin filled with water, and bake for 4 hours at 160°C/325°F/gas mark 3, topping up the water in the roasting tin as necessary.

Invert on to a hot dish and serve in thickish slices. Any left over can be reheated or sliced and fried in a little butter in a non-stick pan.

LYNDA BROWN

Rillons

These irresistible crisp brown squares of belly pork, seen piled high on huge platters in charcuterie windows, are a particular speciality of the Loire. They are very easy to make, and nothing makes finer eating when you're in the mood for something savoury. I keep some permanently in the refrigerator stored under fat. In summer we eat them with salad, in winter with mashed potatoes and apple purée.

Serves 4–6

1.125kg/2½ lb belly pork
1½–2 tsp sea salt
½–1 tsp *quatre épices;* or use mixture of ground cloves,
nutmeg, pepper and either cinnamon or
ginger (optional)

Remove the rind (freeze and save for stews) and cut the meat into roughly 7.5cm/3in squares. Rub with salt, put in a crock or plastic bowl, cover and leave in a cool place for 16–24 hours. Rinse thoroughly and arrange in an ovenproof dish, sprinkling with spice if using (not essential but it does add a lovely flavour). Add water to cover the base of the dish to prevent the meat from sticking, cover and cook in a very low oven (an Aga is ideal), 130°C/250°F/gas mark ½–1, for about 3 hours or until very tender, adding a little extra water if necessary. I have also left them on top of a wood-burning stove overnight, when the stove has been shut down and is just ticking over, which works perfectly.

For immediate consumption, brown in a hot oven or in a non-stick frying pan until nice and crisp. To keep, put in a clean crock, pour in melted lard to cover, cool and refrigerate. Save the cooking juices for the recipe for Pork fillet cooked with prunes and Vouvray, (p. 187).

LYNDA BROWN

Pork fillet with prunes and Vouvray

Pork cooked with prunes soaked in Vouvray is a classic Loire dish. Some recipes are richer than others. This is the version I make at home which does not contain any cream but relies on good stock for its body and flavour. When planning the dish, allow 4–5 days for the prunes to soak until they are ready to use. As this dish only takes about 15 minutes to complete, it makes a good choice for easy entertaining.

Serves 4

4 x 7.5cm/3in lengths of pork tenderloin, trimmed of
skin and membrane
approx. 15–30g/½–1oz butter and 1–2 dsp vegetable oil
for frying
2 Cox's apples, peeled, cored and cut into wedges
8–12 wine-soaked prunes (*see* p. 188)

For the sauce
150ml/5fl. oz well-flavoured stock, preferably veal or
jellied pork stock
150ml/5fl. oz prune liquor from wine-soaked prunes
½ tsp cinnamon or *quatre épices*
7–15g/¼–½ oz unsalted butter, cut into pieces

Brown the meat on both sides over a high heat in a scrap of butter and a little vegetable oil in a non-stick frying pan. Cover and cook gently for 4–5 minutes. Turn off the heat and leave for 5 minutes to complete the cooking. Meanwhile, in a separate pan, fry the apple slices in a little fresh butter and keep hot.

Drain the meat juices into the stock. Reheat the prunes and meat in the frying pan, arrange on hot plates with the apple slices and keep hot while you make the sauce. Add the prune liquor, stock and spices to the pan. Boil hard until the flavour is well balanced (add extra stock if necessary). Off the heat, swirl in pieces of butter to taste and when they have melted pour around the pork. Serve immediately with plain boiled rice.

LYNDA BROWN

Prunes in Vouvray

1 dozen best prunes
55g/2oz sugar
generous 1/2 bottle *demi-sec* Vouvray

Wash the prunes thoroughly in boiling water. Cover with fresh water and soak for 1 hour. Drain. Dissolve the sugar in the wine and pour over the prunes, covering them with wine. Cover and keep in the refrigerator for 4–5 days before using. On their own, they make a luxurious dessert served plain or with a dollop of thick cream. (Quick prunes in brandy, p. 240, can also be served this way.)

LYNDA BROWN

Simone Sekers writes: PRUNES are often coated in mineral oil unless you buy them from wholefood shops. If the oil is unavoidable, rinse them in very hot water and dry on paper towels before cooking.

DESSERTS

Soufflé aux noix

Serves 4

butter for greasing
caster sugar for sprinkling on the dishes
4 sponge finger biscuits
1–2 tbsp Liqueur de Noix or brandy
4 eggs, separated
4 tbsp caster sugar
55g/2oz walnut kernels, finely ground
a little single cream for serving

Break the biscuits into pieces and soak in the liqueur or brandy. Heat the oven to 200°C/400°F/gas mark 6. Butter 4 individual soufflé dishes (11cm/4½in in diameter) or one medium soufflé dish (17.5cm/7in in diameter), and sprinkle the sides and base with caster sugar. Beat the egg yolks with the caster sugar until they become a pale mass. Whip the whites until stiff but not dry. Fold the ground walnuts into the egg yolk mixture and then fold this into the stiff egg whites.

Divide half the mixture between the dishes, add the soaked biscuits, and top with the remaining mixture. Bake in the oven for 15 minutes, then serve at once with a little single cream. A napkin may be wrapped around each dish just before serving to make handling easier.

THANE PRINCE

Tarte Tatin

The most well known of all French apple tarts, Tarte Tatin was made famous by two sisters who ran the Hotel Tatin at Lamotte-Beuvron in the Loire, where the large, handsome Reinette d'Orléans is the major local apple variety. Unlike other apple tarts, the fruit is baked underneath, producing a buttery caramelised and utterly delicious filling. There are many versions of the recipe. This one comes from Claudia Roden.

Serves 8

For the pastry
110g/4oz unsalted butter
185g/6½oz plain flour
2 tbsp caster sugar
1 egg
2–3 tbsp water or milk

For the filling
8 large Cox's Orange Pippins
55g/2oz unsalted butter
5 heaped tbsp sugar
squeeze of lemon

Start with the pastry. Work the butter very well into the flour and sugar, then add the egg and enough water or milk to bind into a soft dough. Wrap and chill for 30 minutes.

For the filling, peel, core and slice the apples. Melt the butter in a 25cm/10in round metal mould or oven tray about 3cm/1¼in deep over a low flame. Add the sugar and lemon and stir until it turns brown. Arrange the apples in a layer of concentric circles over the caramelised butter and sugar, making more layers with the rest of the sliced apples.

Roll the dough out on a floured board with a floured rolling pin and cut a circle to fit inside the tin. Lift it gently and lay it over the apples, pressing down on them lightly. Bake at 230°C/450°F/gas mark 8 for 30 minutes or until lightly browned. Remove it from the oven, cut round the edges and invert it quickly on to a serving dish.

CLAUDIA RODEN

Cherry clafoutis

Serves 5–6

450g/1lb red cherries, stoned
85g/3oz plain flour
85g/3 oz caster sugar
1 tsp salt
4 eggs
600ml/1pt creamy milk
1 tsp vanilla essence

Arrange the fruit in an even layer in a wide, shallow, buttered ovenproof dish. Mix the flour, sugar and salt in a large bowl and make a well in the centre. Beat the eggs into the flour mixture, whisking until there are no lumps. Whisk in the milk and vanilla essence. Pour the batter over the fruit (it should be about 2.5cm/1in deep) and bake in a preheated hot oven, 200°C/400°F/gas mark 6, for 50–60 minutes or until the centre is set. Serve warm.

THANE PRINCE

Editor's note: Other fruits – pears, plums, apricots, or a mixture – can be treated in the same way.

Peach brandy

This recipe comes from a farm deep in rural France. Cut 3–4 sweet ripe peaches in half and place in a deep, wide-necked jar. Sprinkle over 100g/3½ oz caster sugar and pour over half a bottle of brandy. Seal well and leave in a dark place, shaking lightly every so often, for 3 months. The brandy should then be strained and bottled.

The brandy can be used as a liqueur or in champagne cocktails. The peaches can be used in trifles and fruit salads.

THANE PRINCE

ITALY

APPETISERS, SALADS
AND VEGETABLES

Chicken livers on toast

These are called *crostini di fegatini* and are a popular appetiser in Tuscany.

Serves 8

1 medium French bread stick, sliced
225g/8oz chicken livers
3 tbsp olive oil
2 cloves garlic, crushed
4 tbsp Vin Santo (*see* p. 208) or Marsala, or more to taste
5–6 small anchovy fillets
2 tbsp capers
4–5 tiny pickled cucumbers or 1 medium one

Lay the bread out on a tray and toast in the oven at 190°C/375°F/gas mark 5 until golden. Fry the chicken livers gently in the oil with the garlic for about 4–5 minutes until they are brown outside and still pink and juicy inside. Add the rest of the ingredients and blend together to a paste in a food processor. Spread on the toast and serve immediately.

CLAUDIA RODEN

Italian mushrooms in oil Ⓥ

450g/1lb button or other mushrooms
90ml/3fl. oz water
2 tbsp vinegar
1/4 tsp salt
1/2 tsp black peppercorns
1–2 tsp coriander seeds
2 bay leaves
1–2 cloves garlic, or to taste
olive oil

Wipe the mushrooms clean and put them into a saucepan with the water, vinegar, salt, peppercorns and coriander seeds. Bring to the boil and cook for 2 minutes. Drain and dry the mushrooms thoroughly – try not to touch them with your hands. Lift them into sterilised jars (this can be done by putting the jars in the oven for 20 minutes at 150°C/300°F/gas mark 2) with a clean spoon, together with the spices, bay leaves and garlic. Pour over enough oil to cover and seal tightly. Keep for a week before eating.

THANE PRINCE

Tomato and bread salad (Panzanella)

Serves 6

200g/7oz coarse white bread, crusts removed
6 ripe tomatoes
1 red onion
½ cucumber
2 sticks celery
½ bunch basil, shredded
90ml/3fl. oz olive oil
30ml/1fl. oz wine vinegar
salt and pepper

Cut the bread into small pieces. Put in a salad bowl and sprinkle with cold water so that it is moist but not soggy. Add the vegetables, cut into pieces or slices, and the basil. Dress with oil, vinegar, salt and pepper, stir well and leave for half an hour for the bread to absorb the dressing.

CLAUDIA RODEN

Editor's note: It is imperative to use good bread for this favourite Tuscan salad. Tuscan bread is a flavoursome chewy bread, made without salt from unbleached flour. Home-made household bread is the best substitute. Failing that, use one of the speciality white breads made to old-fashioned recipes which produce a denser loaf now available from Marks & Spencer, or an organic white bread such as Safeway sells.

Fried zucchini salad with mint vinaigrette

This recipe, collected by Claudia Roden, comes from the celebrated American chef Joyce Goldstein, who runs her own restaurant, Square One, in San Francisco.

Serves 6

6 medium courgettes, trimmed and cut into
6mm/¼ in rounds
120ml/4fl. oz olive oil
60ml/2fl. oz red wine vinegar
2 tbsp chopped fresh mint
salt and freshly ground black pepper
additional chopped fresh mint

Fry the courgettes in the heated oil in a large frying pan over a medium heat, stirring often, until just tender and lightly browned, about 5 minutes. Transfer to a large bowl, and mix with the vinegar and mint. Season with salt and pepper and cool. Sprinkle with extra mint before serving.

CLAUDIA RODEN

Fresh artichokes

Fresh globe artichokes, a favourite vegetable throughout the Mediterranean, and particularly in Italy, are easier to handle than might be imagined by their appearance. They have the same kind of satisfying texture as waxy potatoes, with a taste somewhere between potatoes and asparagus. Go for ones which look bright and fresh, allowing 1 large or 2 small ones per person. They keep unwrapped in a cool place for over a week (the appearance suffers but the flavour does not). The flesh rapidly discolours, so rub cut surfaces with lemon juice and always cook them in acidulated water in non-reactive pans. Don't, incidentally, be put off by complicated instructions about trimming and 'turning artichokes'. This isn't necessary except for some stuffed dishes. If you need only the hearts, the easiest way is to cook the whole artichoke first, dismantling it as described below.

To cook, soak the artichokes head down in salted water to remove any dirt or insects. Snap off the stalk – this brings away the tough fibres embedded in the heart. Bring a large stainless steel or enamel pan of water to the boil, allowing 1 tbsp of lemon juice or vinegar per 600ml/1pt of water. Add the artichokes and cook steadily for around 35–40 minutes, or until a leaf can be pulled away easily and the flesh at the base is soft. Remove with tongs, and drain them upside down for a few minutes. They retain their heat well, taking up to an hour to cool completely. They can also be cooked in a microwave (consult your book for details) and keep for 2–3 days in the refrigerator.

Whole artichokes are usually eaten warm with melted butter and lemon juice or hollandaise, or cold with mayonnaise, vinaigrette, your favourite dip, or – the Italian way – with a jug of best extra-virgin olive oil, seasoned with salt and pepper. Provide a small bowl of sauce for each person and a huge communal bowl for the debris. To eat, take off the leaves one by one, dip the fleshy base of each leaf into the sauce and eat just this fleshy part. When you get to the central purple pointed cluster of immature leaves which covers the hairy choke (the immature thistle), slice this off with a sharp knife, or pull away with finger and thumb to reveal the tender heart: savour in the same way.

The hearts may also be sliced or diced and used in salads, with pasta, in soups, with meat or fish (prawns and sole especially), in vegetable dishes and in risottos, such as the one that follows on page 205.

LYNDA BROWN

Sicilian-style artichoke, anchovy and caper salad

Allow 1 artichoke heart per person, cooked and cooled as described above. Slice very thinly and arrange on a plate. Squeeze over lemon juice, then trickle over a little good olive oil (lemon olive oil is also lovely; in this case, you will not need any lemon juice). Scatter over some drained capers and decorate with anchovies cut into thin strips, both to taste, and serve.

Variation: Arrange the artichoke hearts as before on individual plates. Squeeze over orange juice, trickle with olive oil, and scatter generously with chopped fresh tarragon, seasoning to taste.

LYNDA BROWN

Simone Sekers writes: ARTICHOKES are a gourmet vegetable when fresh. All I can say about canned artichoke hearts is to quote Jane Grigson – don't use them. They taste canned, whatever you do to them. If labelled artichoke bottoms, then they are in fact very often the hearts, with a squashy and unattractive texture. Good Italian delicatessens sell artichoke hearts in olive oil as an ingredient for an antipasto, very often beautifully arranged with red peppers, stuffed olives and neatly rolled anchovies in tall glass jars, looking like a mosaic from Pompeii. These are good but expensive, and so decorative it is almost a pity to eat them. If you grow your own artichokes and have a glut of smallish ones, they are easily prepared, blanched and then frozen – which works very well. Vacuum-packed artichoke hearts (often used in restaurants) are becoming available, though I have not tried them yet.

Aubergines baked with tomatoes and cheese

This dish appears in various guises all over Italy, usually with several layers of aubergines. This version is Claudia Roden's favourite.

Serves 4

2 large aubergines, sliced
salt
olive oil for deep-frying

For the tomato sauce
1 clove garlic, crushed
2 tbsp olive oil
450g/1lb ripe tomatoes, peeled and chopped
1 tsp sugar
bunch of basil or mint leaves, chopped
salt and pepper

To finish
1–2 mozzarella cheeses (approx. 110g/4oz each), diced
(*see* p. 200)
4 tbsp grated Parmesan cheese

Salt the aubergine slices and leave for half an hour to let the juices run out. Rinse, drain and pat dry. Deep-fry in hot oil for 3–4 minutes, turning over once, and drain on kitchen paper. Meanwhile, make the tomato sauce. Fry the garlic in the olive oil until the aroma rises. Add the tomatoes, sugar, herbs and a little salt and pepper and cook vigorously to reduce, about 15–20 minutes.

Arrange the aubergine slices in an ovenproof dish or baking tray, cover with the tomato sauce, sprinkle with the cheeses and bake in a moderate oven, 180°C/350°F/gas mark 4, for about 30 minutes.

CLAUDIA RODEN

Simone Sekers writes: PARMESAN CHEESE is often badly used in this country – the tubs of ready-grated cheese do not deserve space in any cupboard, particularly since fresh Parmesan is widely available in supermarkets. It also keeps very well in the least cold part of the refrigerator, improving its cooking qualities as it ages – Italians think that we use it as a cooking cheese while it is still too young. At a year or so old, they serve it as a dessert cheese, at 18 months old it is used for grating, with the *stravecchio*, at 2 years old or more, kept for cooking. For convenience, buy it in large quantities, grate it (easily done in a food processor), then freeze it in useful quantities – about 110g/4oz at a time. I find that this does compromise the flavour somewhat, although it is better than the sawdust in tubs. Parmegiano-reggiano is the regional Parmesan most often found in this country, but there are other *grano* cheeses which do as well. Peccorino, a semi-hard ewe's-milk cheese, is almost as good as a pasta and a dessert cheese, and often cheaper. Not often found in supermarkets, it is more often to be seen on cheese counters in good food shops and Italian delicatessens.

Baked potatoes with rosemary and garlic ⓥ

This is a simple and most delicious way of preparing potatoes.

Serves 4

900g/2lb new potatoes
salt and pepper
3–4 cloves garlic, crushed
5 tbsp olive oil
leaves from 2 or more sprigs of rosemary, chopped

Scrub the potatoes well and boil in salted water until tender. Drain, cut them in half if they are large and put with the rest of the ingredients in a baking dish, turning them to cover them well with the oil and the aromatics. Bake at 200°C/400°F/gas mark 6 for 20 minutes or until golden.

CLAUDIA RODEN

See also: Italian olive and mushroom sauce for pasta, p. 102.

PIZZA

In the past 20 years, pizza has become the world's staple fast food. Traditionally, it is baked directly on the bottom of a searingly hot wood-fired oven. Within 3 or 4 minutes the pizza is cooked, the base blistered and crisp, the topping melted yet still juicy. A home-made pizza cannot compare with one made in this way, but, provided that the oven is hot and a few simple rules are followed, a home-made pizza can be very good indeed and certainly far better than any of the commercial ones you can buy.

Though simple, ingredients are important. The best pizzas require fruity olive oil, creamy mozzarella, plump olives and anchovies, ripe tomatoes or their tinned equivalent, fresh basil and oregano. Pizza dough is easy to make and freezes well. Knock back after it has risen and freeze in plastic bags. Thaw, roll or shape the dough as required and proceed in the manner described below. This recipe for genuine Neapolitan pizza, and the variations that follow, are from Claudia Roden.

Pizza dough

Makes 4 x 23cm/9in individual pizzas

450g/1lb unbleached plain or bread flour, plus extra
flour for flouring the board and rolling pin
1/4 tsp salt
30g/1oz fresh or 15g/1/2 oz dried yeast
pinch sugar
5 tbsp olive oil
300ml/10fl. oz lukewarm water

Put the flour into a bowl with the salt. Dissolve the yeast in half a glass of the measured water, with a pinch of sugar to activate the yeast (if you use 'active' dried yeast it can go straight into the flour dry – follow the instructions on the packet). When the yeast froths, pour it into the flour. Add 3 tbsp of the oil and just enough water to make a firm dough. Pour the water in gradually, mixing first with a wooden spoon, then working the flour into the liquid with your hands. Add a little more flour if it is too sticky.

Knead well for 10 minutes or until the dough is smooth and elastic. Pour a drop of oil in the bowl and roll the dough in it to prevent a dry crust forming on the surface. Cover with a damp cloth (or enclose in a plastic bag) and leave to rise in a warm place for about an hour or until the dough has doubled in bulk. Punch it down and knead for a few minutes more, then roll it in a little oil again.

Now divide the dough into 4 balls and roll them out on a floured board with a lightly floured rolling pin. Push the dough with your hands to stretch it. Lift the rounds carefully and transfer them to two oiled baking sheets. Spread the filling ingredients (see following list for suggestions) evenly on top and bake in the hottest part of a preheated oven, 230–250°C/450–475°F/gas mark 8–9, for about 20–25 minutes or until the edges and bottom are crisp. Serve at once.

Editor's note: Olive oil enriches the dough and adds a little extra flavour, but is not essential and you can reduce the amount or leave it out if you prefer.

Neapolitan fillings

Quantities are for a single pizza

Pomodoro e formaggio: Cover the dough with 2 tinned peeled tomatoes, chopped and with the juice squeezed out, 1 heaped tbsp of grated Parmesan (*see* p. 197), salt and pepper, chopped parsley or garlic.

Margherita: Spread 2–3 tinned peeled tomatoes, chopped and with their juice squeezed out, over the dough, cover with 85g/3oz mozzarella, sliced or diced, and sprinkle with 1 heaped tbsp of grated Parmesan (*see* p. 197), salt and pepper, 1 crushed clove of garlic, a few basil leaves and 2 tbsp oil.

Margherita bianca: Brush the dough with 2 tbsp of olive oil, cover with a few slices of mozzarella and sprinkle with salt, pepper, 1 heaped tbsp of grated Parmesan (*see* p. 197) and a few basil leaves.

Alla Romana: Add to the above filling a few chopped anchovy fillets.

Alla Marinara: Spread 2 tinned and peeled chopped tomatoes, squeezed of their juice, on the dough and sprinkle with 2–3 tbsp of capers, a few black olives (*see* p. 117), a few chopped anchovies, 2 tbsp olive oil, salt and pepper.

CLAUDIA RODEN

Editor's note: My own method of making pizza is slightly different. Because domestic ovens do not have the required intensity of bottom heat, a home-made pizza is cooked for far longer than a commercial one.

To prevent the filling drying up or the cheese becoming too browned, I prefer to bake the dough without the filling for 10 minutes first, then spread the filling on top, return the pizza to the oven and cook it for another 7–10 minutes until the filling is hot and the cheese melted and beginning to bubble. I find this method works perfectly every time, producing a nice crisp base and a moist topping.

A couple more points are worth making. The pizza base should be thin, no more than 6mm/¼ in thick, with a thicker rim around the outside. Purpose-made pizza tins, which are readily available, are what I prefer to use, and I shape the dough directly on to the oiled tins, pushing and patting it out with my knuckles and hands rather than rolling it first. Once shaped, it is important to let the dough relax for a while, anything up to 45 minutes or so, before you bake it – this helps to make a puffy, well-risen pizza. Baking the pizza on a preheated baking sheet also helps to give a boost of bottom heat. Put the baking sheet into the oven when you switch the oven on and leave it there when you take the pizza out to spread the filling on top.

The tomatoes, or any moist topping, must be well drained or the base of the pizza will be soggy. A simple tomato sauce made with tinned or fresh tomatoes, sliced onion, perhaps a clove of crushed garlic and 1 dsp of tomato purée makes a good topping, cooked until it is very thick, then sieved through a mouli and with plenty of chopped oregano (or 1 tsp dried *rigani, see* p. 120) stirred in. If you parbake the pizza first as I have recommended, warm the tomato sauce through before spreading it on the pizza.

A pizza must be served as soon as it is ready, sizzling hot. If you make a large pizza, or extra for seconds (I have never known anyone not eat more pizza), keep any left over on the warming tray – this crisps up the base even more as well as keeping the pizza hot.

Simone Sekers writes: MOZZARELLA has rocketed to stardom with the rise of the pizza. It is also used, too often with flavourless tomatoes, both straight from the refrigerator, as a poor apology for a salad which can be delicious. True mozzarella is snowy-white and made from buffalo milk, and has a creamier, more refined and delicate flavour than that made from cow's milk. Unfortunately, it is the latter, cheaper sort that we find most easily in this country, although good Italian delicatessens stock the real thing, which should be reserved for salads.

For pizzas, cow's milk mozzarella is better. Beware of that which looks and feels hard and rubbery (avoid, too, grated packet mozzarella if you can, which is often inferior). Good mozzarella should be moist and creamy and look fresh. It is widely available, though an Italian delicatessen is likely to have a rapid turnover, and so the mozzarella is likely to be fresher. The best type for pizza are brands made by Italians in this country such as Olympia and Carnevale. Both grated mozzarella and whole mozzarella, sliced and cut into sticks, may be marinated in olive oil before being used on pizzas. It freezes well; there is some loss of texture but the cooking quality is unaltered.

POLENTA

Polenta is made from maize meal (also called cornmeal), and is the staple food of northern Italy. Depending on the region or personal taste, it can be made in various ways – soft and creamy, or firm enough to be cut into slices, then grilled or fried. It makes an admirable alternative to potatoes, pasta or rice to accompany rich braises and stews, or for simple grills, or to accompany vegetarian dishes. Char-grilled until crisp, it has become a popular restaurant food to serve with game or sausages, with fish dishes, or on its own with a fresh tomato and basil sauce and Parmesan cheese. Once tried, like me, you could become addicted!

Traditionally, polenta is made by simmering cornmeal and water on top of the stove, stirring constantly until it is ready, when it becomes elastic and comes away cleanly from the side of the pan. A modern way of cooking polenta, however, which is easier and works very well, is to bake it in the oven, as in the following recipe from Claudia Roden.

Baked polenta

Serves 6–8

285g/10oz maize meal (cornmeal)
1.5l/2½ pt water
2 tsp salt

Put the maize meal with the cold water in a very large saucepan (it needs space to swell by more than a third) and stir thoroughly until no lumps remain. Add the salt and, stirring vigorously and constantly so that lumps do not form (this is crucial), bring to the boil slowly. Cook for 5 minutes or so, stirring, then pour into a greased baking tray or bowl. Aim for a layer about 2.5cm/1in thick. Cover tightly with foil and bake in the oven at 180°C/350°F/gas mark 4 for about 1–1½ hours. A golden crust will form on top and it will be soft underneath. Let it rest for a few minutes before serving. A mixture of milk and water can also be used, which produces a creamier-tasting polenta.

To make *crostoni*, let it cool and become firm, then cut into slices and toast under the grill till lightly browned on both sides. Or brown in a frying pan in a little butter or olive oil.

Polenta a boconi is served in deep bowls with plenty of butter and grated Parmesan (*see* p. 197). For sweet *polenta a boconi dolce*, sprinkle with sugar and cinnamon instead of Parmesan.

CLAUDIA RODEN

Editor's note: How stiff or soft polenta becomes depends on the quantity of liquid used. It can vary from being a very stiff, almost granular paste to having a soft, custard-like consistency. Either way is very good, and it depends purely on how you like it and what it is being served with. The amount of liquid used in this recipe produces a softish, medium-stiff polenta. Rather than trying to remember specific quantities of water, a useful working guide is to use simple ratios of polenta to water. For a stiff polenta which forms a paste and which can be turned out and cut into wedges for frying and grilling, use 1 part polenta to 4 parts water. This takes only 15 minutes or so to cook on top of the stove, or 30–40 minutes in the oven, baked as described above. If you want a soft, smooth polenta, use 1 part polenta to 6 parts water, allowing a little extra cooking time in the oven if necessary. All polentas firm up on cooling, and are best eaten warm rather than very hot. If you do not like salt, or need to reduce salt intake for health reasons, reduce the quantity accordingly; it can even be left out, which is what I prefer myself.

Simone Sekers writes: POLENTA is best bought from Italian delicatessens. Some of that sold in wholefood shops is rather too fine – the grains should look like yellow powdered glass, which produces a tastier polenta. Look for packets labelled cornmeal (maize flour, which is finer, and milled from different varieties of corn, is used for breads, and is not really suitable for polenta), available either coarse or fine-ground. Both are suitable.

GNOCCHI, RISOTTO AND
OTHER ITALIAN CLASSICS

Potato dumplings (Gnocchi di patata) (√)

These, writes Claudia Roden, are another northern Italian speciality: 'They are especially popular in Friuli, the area of Italy bordering Austria and Yugoslavia, where they make them in all shapes and sizes – in little balls the size of peas or large walnuts, and also in squares, ovals and fingers. After much experimenting I found that baking rather than boiling the potatoes results in perfect gnocchi which never fail. Because there is less moisture they need less flour and taste purely of potato. Use floury rather than waxy potatoes, such as King Edwards.'

Serves 4

675g/1½ lb weighed baked potato flesh (allow about
900g/2lb potatoes)
salt
2 egg yolks
100g/3½ oz plain flour

For the dressing
55g/2oz melted butter
grated Parmesan cheese (*see* p. 197)

The potatoes should be the same size. Wash and bake them in their jackets (not in foil as it makes them retain too much moisture) in the oven, 200°C/400°F/gas mark 6, for an hour or until soft.

Peel, weigh and mash them while still hot so that they are very smooth, without any lumps. Season with salt, work in the egg yolks and flour, and knead well to a smooth elastic doughy paste. Now shape the paste into little balls: the usual way is to make long rolls the thickness of a thumb and cut them into 2cm/¾in segments. Press these against a grater or the prongs of a fork to mark them, so that they hold the dressing better. Place them so that they do not touch on a floured cloth.

Cook the gnocchi in batches in a large pan half full of barely simmering water for at least 10 minutes. Lift them out of the water with a slotted spoon, drain well and serve with melted butter and a sprinkling of cheese.

Variations: 1 tsp of cinnamon is sometimes dusted on.

Gnocchi are often served with the sauce from a meat or duck stew. *Veneto-style* gnocchi are served with 450g/1lb peeled and chopped tomatoes heated in a pan with 2 tbsp of butter, seasoned with salt and pepper, and finished with a sprinkling of chopped parsley – with grated cheese passed around.

CLAUDIA RODEN

Quail with fried sage leaves and artichoke risotto

This is a feast of a dish. Getting risotto right, creamy and just spreading a little on the plate, is a question of judgement. The secret is to stir the rice often and not to overcook it. It must be served immediately. If you need to delay, stop the cooking halfway through – a good tip to know if getting everybody to the table on time is tricky. Most of the preparation can be done well in advance, leaving just the final cooking which takes no more than about 25 minutes.

Serves 4

8 fresh oven-ready quail
8 large sprigs sage
1–2 tbsp olive oil
4–5 tbsp dry white wine

For the risotto
3 large or 4 medium globe artichokes, cooked
(see p. 194–5)
7–15g/¼–½ oz butter
1 tbsp olive oil
1 small onion, finely chopped
300g/10oz arborio rice
salt
150ml/5fl. oz dry white wine
approx. 750–850ml/1¼–1½ pt hot chicken stock
a little extra butter

Wipe the quail, rub them with sage and put 2–3 sage leaves in each cavity. Truss up the legs and reserve.

Next, dismantle the artichokes (this can be done in advance, if necessary). Peel off the outer leaves and, using a teaspoon, scrape out the flesh from the leaf bases and reserve. Remove the inner purple pointed cluster of leaves to reveal the hairy choke (the immature thistle). Slice off the choke with a sharp knife, or remove by pulling it out with your finger and thumb to reveal the artichoke heart. Dice and reserve.

For the risotto, heat the butter and olive oil in a large heavy pan (Le Creuset is ideal), and gently soften the onion in it. Add the rice, then the reserved artichoke flesh, and stir to coat well. Season lightly with salt, add the diced artichoke hearts and wine. Cook until the wine has evaporated, then start adding the hot stock, a glassful at a time. Cook gently, stirring often, adding more stock as it becomes absorbed, until the rice is just soft and the risotto is creamy, about 20–25 minutes. Do not cook past this stage – the residual heat will continue to cook the risotto. Check the seasoning, dot with a few flakes of butter, and give a final stir.

Start cooking the quail at the same time as the risotto. Brown all over in the olive oil over a highish heat in a non-stick pan. Add the sprigs of sage to the pan, turn down the heat, cover and cook gently for 15–20 minutes, turning the quail often. They should be well browned and crisp. Remove the cover, turn up the heat to finish crisping, splash with the wine, and cook for another minute or so. Put the cover back to keep warm if necessary.

Pile the risotto on to a hot serving platter. Arrange the quail, fried sage and any meat juices around the sides, decorate with fresh sage and serve immediately, with a plain green salad.

LYNDA BROWN

Simone Sekers writes: ARBORIO RICE, which has no substitute, is the generic name for the rice grown in the Piedmont region of northern Italy. The grains are shorter and fatter than ordinary long-grain rice, and their thin outer layer dissolves readily to allow the grains to absorb liquid and flavour, without becoming soft too quickly. It therefore takes slightly longer to cook, and produces the correct, slightly sticky texture of a true Italian risotto. It is available in most supermarkets. For the more interesting variations such as Carnaroli, Roma and Baldo, you will have to go to an Italian delicatessen.

Chicken croquettes

Serve these as part of a *fritto misto* or with fried potatoes.

Serves 4 or more

285g/10oz boiled boned chicken or leftover cooked
chicken meat
stiff béchamel sauce made with 30g/1oz butter,
2 tbsp flour and 300ml/10fl. oz milk
1 egg
3 tbsp grated Parmesan cheese (*see* p. 197)
pinch of nutmeg
salt and pepper
breadcrumbs for coating
oil for deep-frying

Finely chop the chicken (you may use a food processor) and put into a bowl with the béchamel, egg, Parmesan, nutmeg, salt and pepper. Mix well, shape into little round cakes, dip in breadcrumbs and deep-fry in oil until golden. Drain well on kitchen paper and serve hot.

Note: To make béchamel sauce, melt the butter in a saucepan, stir in the flour and very gradually add the milk, previously infused with onion, bay leaf and peppercorns, stirring constantly and waiting until it boils before adding more. Then cook very gently, stirring often, until the sauce thickens.

CLAUDIA RODEN

See also: Pheasant in red wine, p. 89; Chicken with rosemary, p. 34.

Lorenza de' Medici's grape bread

This recipe comes from the Badia a Coltibuono estate, near Radda in Tuscany, famous for its wine and olive oil and home of the Italian cookery writer Lorenza de' Medici. Serve warm, cut into wedges with tea or coffee as a pastry, or to accompany barbecued food.

2 tbsp fresh yeast, or 2 packets active dried yeast
150ml/5fl. oz lukewarm milk
310g/11oz plain unbleached flour
140g/5oz sugar
450g/1lb black grapes, washed, seeded, skin left on
200g/7oz raisins soaked overnight in Vin Santo or other
sweet dessert wine and drained
salt

If using fresh yeast, dissolve it in the lukewarm milk. If using dried yeast, add to any dry ingredients, leaving the milk to the end. Mound the flour in a large bowl with a well in the centre. Add 100g/3½oz sugar and a pinch of salt, and stir in the yeast/milk mixture. Mix well and knead for 5 minutes, then cover with a clean cloth and leave in a warm place to rise until doubled in size.

Punch down and shape into two rounds about 20cm/8in across. Place one on a floured baking sheet, cover with half the grapes and half the drained raisins. Cover with the second round of dough, and on top put the rest of the grapes and raisins. Leave covered to rise again until doubled in size. Sprinkle with the rest of the sugar and bake in a preheated oven, 180°C/350°F/gas mark 4, for about 45 minutes.

CLAUDIA RODEN

Simone Sekers writes: VIN SANTO is a curious, heavy, sweet oxidised and very alcoholic Italian wine (specified in this recipe because it is a speciality of the house of Badia a Coltibuono). Madeira, Marsala or sweet sherry will all pass as substitutes.

DESSERTS

Italians like to finish their meal with something simple like fresh fruit. They are also well known for their marvellous granitas and sorbets. Here are two from Claudia Roden, the well-known coffee granita from Sicily, and a sensational creamy apricot ice.

Coffee granita

Serves 8

1l/1½ pt good strong coffee
4 tbsp sugar or to taste
300ml/10fl. oz whipped cream (optional)

Dissolve the sugar in the coffee while it is hot (it is best made not too sweet). Let it cool, then pour into ice cube trays. Cover with cling film, and put in the freezer for several hours. Allowing 2–3 ice cubes per person, just before serving, whizz the ice cubes in a food processor to a soft or crunchy consistency. Serve immediately, piled into glasses, topped, if you like, with cream.   CLAUDIA RODEN

Apricot ice

Serves 6

450g/1lb very ripe apricots, pitted

For the syrup
100g/3½ oz sugar, or more to taste
210ml/7fl. oz water
Juice of 1 lemon
1–2 tbsp orange-flower water (optional)

Boil the sugar and water until the sugar melts (the amount depends on the sweetness of the fruit), add the lemon juice and let the syrup cool a little, then blend with the apricots to a cream, adding the orange-flower water if using. Pour into ice-cube freezer trays, cover with cling film or foil and freeze for a few hours until hard.

Just before serving, put the frozen apricot cubes through the food processor, a few at a time, and blend to a very soft cream. You can put the ice-cream in a serving bowl and return it to the freezer, covered until a few minutes before you are ready to serve.   CLAUDIA RODEN

Simone Sekers writes: ORANGE-FLOWER WATER is distilled from the flowers of the bitter or Seville orange, and is an essential flavouring to keep in the store cupboard, along with rose-water. It is available in concentrated form, too, sometimes labelled as 'triple strength', from delicatessens, good grocers and kitchen shops. Add it cautiously, drop by drop, tasting as you go, to fruit salads, sorbets, sponge-cake mixtures and cream fillings for cakes, meringues and pavlovas.

Ricotta ice-cream

Ricotta, writes Claudia Roden, is the basis of many Italian sweets: 'It is sometimes eaten mixed with ground coffee and sugar or with honey and cinnamon. This ice-cream is a modern and popular way of using it. It is good served with fruits in wine or syrup.'

Serves 6–8

5 egg yolks
100g/3½ oz caster sugar
5 tbsp rum, cognac, or to taste
450g/1lb fresh ricotta

Start by putting the egg yolks in a blender with the sugar and blend till pale and fluffy. Then add the rum or cognac followed by the ricotta, and blend to a light cream. Line a mould with cling film or foil, pour in the mixture and cover with another piece of cling film or foil. Leave in the freezer for at least three hours. To serve, remove the lining and turn out on to a plate.

CLAUDIA RODEN

Simone Sekers writes: RICOTTA is a bland, slightly sweet milky-white soft cheese made from whey mixed with milk. It is used in many Italian pasta and sweet dishes. Available from Italian shops, some supermarkets and most delicatessens, it is usually moulded in the form of an upturned pudding basin. Since it is a low-fat cheese with a high moisture content it does not keep well, so make sure it is fresh by trying a little before buying. If it is stale it will have an unpleasant 'off' flavour. It can also be bought in vacuum-packed 450g/1lb bags which are useful, but check their sell-by date before buying.

See also: Sicilian cheesecake, p. 237; Zabaglione, p. 172.

Christmas

SINCE VICTORIAN TIMES, Christmas has been the most important festival in our calendar, the time when good cheer and good food and wine are to be had in plenty. It is also the busiest time in the kitchen, with preparations beginning a month in advance, often culminating in frenzied activity on the great day itself. The pleasure of cooking the traditional feast and entertaining on a grander than usual scale is matched against the challenge of finding new ways of presenting familiar themes, or of simply finding time to do them at all.

In the main – as someone pointed out to me recently – Christmas Day itself runs on well-oiled lines in the kitchen. It is therefore not the intention of this chapter to tell you how to roast a turkey or make a Christmas pudding, but rather to bring together a collection of appropriate recipes, built around seasonal produce, which will stand you in good stead over the festive season.

A modern Christmas takes the best of the old and the best of the new. Increasingly, I find, the real pleasure of Christmas lies less in overloading the system with rich food than in concentrating on the best ingredients you can find: wild smoked salmon from a specialist supplier, a proper free-range turkey, and some genuine farmhouse cheeses. All are available through mail order (one of the easiest and best ways to do the Christmas shopping) and are, happily, becoming easier to find as small producers proliferate and flourish. Unusual jams and jellies, preserved meats, smoked delicacies, real kippers sent from Scotland, hand-made chocolates, fine teas and coffees make the best gifts, too. I'm sure this is the way modern Christmases will develop, and it gives me great pleasure to include on pp. 216–7 a few of the best, selected by Simone Sekers.

TRADITIONAL CHRISTMAS FARE

If the thought of all that rich food appals rather than appeals, but you are loath to abandon traditional fare, try leaving most of the fat out of both the pudding and mincemeat (see recipe on p. 219). All that suet is just a remnant of the former meat content of such dishes and isn't necessary – vegetable suet isn't much of a substitute. I make my mincemeat about a fortnight before Christmas, lace it well with alcohol and store it in the refrigerator if the weather is warm. The pudding is made a month before and keeps perfectly well. Since both of these have been divested of their fat, I can relax over the pastry for the mince pies, using half butter (for flavour) and half vegetable lard (for lightness). I make brandy butter using twice as much butter as sugar (it is usually the other way round), melting unsalted butter over a low heat and stirring in soft brown sugar and a sherry glass of brandy to each 225g/8oz butter. Once all this has been well mixed, take a pan off the heat and sit aside to cool. Stir the contents briskly as it cools and the butter begins to set, and when it is a good homogeneous mixture, spoon it into a decorative pot that can appear at the table. It is a good idea to supply thick cream for those who don't want to add more alcohol, but it must be good cream. Clotted cream can be bought by post for Christmas (see below) and is delicious with the dark, fruity pudding.

Brussels sprouts really do go well with turkey, and here is a trouble-free way of preparing them. Trim and cook them on Christmas Eve. On Christmas Day, chop the sprouts very roughly with a heavy knife – they shouldn't be reduced to a purée, but should be left quite chunky. Heat a generous lump of butter in a heavy pan, together with 1 tbsp of coarse-grain mustard to each 450g/1lb sprouts. Reheat the chopped sprouts very gently in this mixture – they can be doing this unattended provided the heat is low enough, while you eat the first course. If mustard is likely to be too alien a flavour, try adding finely chopped celery leaves (those nice pale yellow ones from the heart) instead.

It is best to buy fresh rather than a frozen turkey, and preferably from a farm where they raise their own. If you like the firmer texture and more pronounced flavour of a free-range bird, then order this well in advance. If you do have to take delivery of a fresh bird at a time when there is no more space in the refrigerator, then store it in an insulated bag, surrounded by relays of ice packs. The stuffing can be made well ahead and frozen. The length of time it takes to defrost is partly determined by what proportion of meat there is to breadcrumbs in its composition: the higher the proportion of bread, the more quickly it will thaw. It must be fully defrosted before you stuff the turkey. If your stuffing recipe contains chestnuts, avoid the fiddly peeling by buying dried ones – which need a long soak – or those packed in vacuum-sealed cans.

If you choose to have a goose (*see* pp. 224–5) instead of a turkey, it is always well to remember that it doesn't have as much meat on it, and there will be fewer leftovers to see you through Boxing Day and for sandwiches for the feature film, and so on. Be prepared to buy a large piece of gammon as well, and cook it 2 days ahead so that it can fill those gaps. It can also be made into useful quick dishes such as *salade cauchoise* (equal quantities of cubed ham, cubed cooked potato and diced celery, none of these too fine, dressed with vinaigrette made with virgin olive oil and sprinkled with parsley), or used as an omelette filling, or to add to a pasta sauce (*see also* Jambalaya, p. 234).

Buy parsley, watercress, chicory, radicchio and Chinese leaves to fill the salad drawer of the refrigerator. Salads lighten the Christmas diet considerably, but lettuce, cucumber and tomatoes are all at their worst (make the Chinese cabbage and sharon fruit salad on p. 222 instead). Celery keeps well out of the refrigerator if wrapped in damp newspaper and stored on a cold floor, and, together with diced unpeeled Cox's apples and some watercress leaves, makes a perfect salad to partner the dryish meat from the turkey's ample breast.

A fresh pineapple looks wonderful as part of the festive sideboard, and makes a welcome alternative to pudding and mincepies.

SIMONE SEKERS

MAIL ORDER FOR CHRISTMAS

Shopping for high-quality provisions for Christmas can be time-consuming if you only have a supermarket as provider. The following firms provide interesting alternatives:

Smoked wild salmon: Ashdown Smokers, Skellerah Farm, Corney, Cumberland LA19 5TW. Tel. 065 78 324.

Smoked salmon trout: Inverawe Smokehouses, Taynuilt, Argyll PA35 1HU. Tel. 08662 446, fax 08662 274.

Both these firms offer other smoked delicacies – kippers, game and so forth.

Real farmhouse cheese, British, Irish, French, Italian, Dutch and Swiss: Wells Stores (Streatley) Ltd, Streatley, nr Reading, Berkshire RG8 9HY. Tel. 0491 872367.

Clotted cream: A. E. Rodda & Son, The Creamery, Scorrier, nr Redruth, Cornwall TR16 5BU. Tel. (0209) 820526.

Ham, bacon, sausages and salami, all made from organic meat: Swaddles Green Farm, Hare Lane, Buckland St Mary, Chard, Somerset TA20 3JR. Tel. 046 034 387.

Fresh meat, poultry and game, conservation grade and superlatively prepared ready to cook: The Pure Meat Company, Moretonhampstead, Devon. Tel. 0647 40321, fax 0647 40402.

Cakes, including variations suitable for vegans or vegetarians: Meg Rivers Cakes, Middle Tysoe, Warwickshire CV35 0SE. Tel. 0295 88 8101, fax 0295 88 799.

Organic Fruit Cake, Christmas pudding; Cumberland Rum Nicky and other wholefood specialities: Village Bakery Melmerby, Penrith, Cumbria CA10 1HE. Tel. 0768 881515.

Chocolates, Belgian fresh cream truffles: S'il Vous Plait, 3 Field End, Crendon Industrial Estate, Long Crendon, Aylesbury, Bucks HP18 9BB. 24-hour hotline 0844 201690, fax 0844 201680.

Chocolates, hand-made on the premises: Humphreys, 16 Leeds Road, Ilkley, West Yorkshire LS29 8DJ. Tel. 0943 609477.

Special teas, coffees, and speciality cakes: Betty's by Post, 1 Parliament Street, Harrogate HG1 2QU. Tel. 0423 531211, fax 0423 565191.

Coffees: Intercoffee, 84 High Street, Tonbridge, Kent TN9 1AP. Tel. 0732 770657.

For the ultimate Christmas hamper, full of local delicacies and products from her own rare breed pigs, contact Anne Petch: Heal Farm, Kings Nympton, Umberleigh, Devon EX37 9TB. Tel. 07695 2077/4341, fax 07695 2837.

Smoked salmon

It is almost impossible to recommend one brand of smoked salmon more highly than another. It really does depend on whether you like a mild cure (salmon smoked in London rather than Scotland will give you this), or an aromatic cure, in which case you should go to one or other of the small specialist smokehouses (see addresses on p. 216). Pinneys, a long-established firm near Dumfries, produce a good middle-of-the-road flavour for Marks & Spencer, together with a special method of trimming each slice to remove the dark brown 'V' of flesh that can be tough and often tastes oily. Smoked salmon trout is a good alternative to salmon, although it is often no cheaper. The best way to serve it, despite all the recipes that have been devised, is very simply, with good brown bread spread with slightly salted butter, and generous quarters of a thin-skinned, juicy lemon.

SIMONE SEKERS

Cheese

Christmas is the one time of the year when everybody buys more cheese than usual, or receives an unexpected Stilton or truckle of Cheddar as a gift. It is also an ideal opportunity to try some of the many excellent genuine British farmhouse cheeses, now available by mail order from cheese specialists such as Neal's Yard Dairy in Covent Garden in London or Wells Stores in Streatley, who will parcel you up a selection in prime condition in good time for Christmas. Whole cheeses, large or small, are especially appealing, and, looked after properly, remain in good condition for 3–4 weeks. To get the best out of them, they should be cut carefully (the practice of digging a spoon into Stilton is to be abhorred). At home, we slice off the top crust, and remove a 'wheel' of cheese for eating by slicing across again. The crust is then replaced, which helps to prevent the cheese from drying out, and the cheese keeps its appearance intact and does not end up looking like something which has been attacked from all sides. The best accompaniment to cheese, especially if you are drinking wine or port, is an apple, which cleanses the palate and is a natural partner for both.

Good cheese is not cheap, so it pays to know how to store it properly. Here is Simone Sekers' advice.

Storing cheeses: Ideally, cheese should not be stored in the refrigerator, but wrapped in damp muslin in a cold larder. Most of us, however, tend to have warm kitchens and no larders, so there is no alternative to the refrigerator. If this is the case with you, choose the shelf furthest from the ice-making compartment. Conversely, if you have a larder fridge, then usually the top shelf is the least cold. Wrap each piece well in waxed or greaseproof paper, line a polythene box with a damp napkin and put the cheese in this. If possible, remove the cheese at least an hour before serving, in order to allow it to warm up to room temperature. Cheese freezes *quite* well, for short periods, but should be wrapped very thoroughly as the intense cold makes it dry out (there will also be some loss of texture over time). Remove these wrappings before defrosting, or the cheese will get very damp.

SIMONE SEKERS

Mincemeat

Mincemeat dates from the Middle Ages and, as its name implies, was originally a heavily spiced minced meat mixture, usually of beef or lamb. This may sound strange to modern tastes, but a little minced meat, say 55g/2oz lean minced steak or lamb for every 450g/1lb of mincemeat adds an extra richness without detracting from its essential flavour.

Over the years I have come to realise that ingredients and proportions can be varied to suit. This is the version that has evolved in my kitchen. It has less sugar than traditional recipes and hardly any fat, but is convivially boozy.

Makes approx. 790g/1³/₄lb

225g/8oz good-flavoured apples, e.g. Cox's, weighed
after peeling and coring
255g/9oz currants
85g/3oz chopped sultanas
30g/1oz flaked almonds, chopped (optional)
30–45g/1¹/₂ oz suet or melted butter
55g/2oz dark sugar
2 tbsp coarse marmalade, chopped (instead of candied
peel, and better)
75–90ml/2¹/₂–3fl. oz brandy
scrubbed rind and juice of ¹/₂ lemon
¹/₄–¹/₂ tsp *quatre épices* or mixed spice
¹/₂ freshly grated nutmeg

Chop the apples into very small bits in a food processor or by hand and mix all the ingredients together in a roomy bowl. Check for taste, adding extra sugar/spices/lemon/marmalade if necessary, and pot. This can be used immediately or stored for up to a year in sterilised and sealed jars.

LYNDA BROWN

FINGER FOOD, OR canapés, is the stock-in-trade of Christmas drinks parties. As a change from the usual things on sticks, here are two ideas from Claudia Roden, served hot. The first, a *tapas* dish from Spain, also makes an admirable quick and easy supper or dinner dish served with rice, or salad and bread. The liver and kidneys can be prepared in advance and kept covered in the refrigerator, but do not roll them in flour until the time comes to cook them.

Liver and kidneys in sherry sauce

Serves 6

225g/8oz calves' or lamb's kidneys
225g/8oz chicken livers
flour for dusting
2 large tomatoes, peeled, de-seeded and chopped
1 clove garlic
120ml/4fl. oz dry sherry
3 tbsp olive or sunflower oil for frying
salt and pepper
pinch ground nutmeg

Cut out the tough cores from the kidneys, snip the membranes and rinse briefly, then cut into bite-sized pieces. Pull off the veins from the livers and separate the two halves. Season both with salt, pepper and nutmeg and roll in flour to seal in the juices.

Meanwhile, simmer the tomatoes with the whole garlic clove and sherry for about 10 minutes or until the sauce is reduced and thick. Sauté the kidneys and livers for 1–2 minutes in hot oil, putting the kidneys in first. The livers should remain pink inside. Lift them out of the oil and add them to the sauce. Heat through, stirring gently. Remove the garlic clove before serving. Eat with forks.

CLAUDIA RODEN

Cheese cigarettes ⓥ

These pretty and delicious little cheese rolls from Turkey are usually deep fried, writes Claudia Roden, but it is lighter and far better to bake them and serve them crisp and hot from the oven. Filo pastry is sold in 450g/1lb boxes, so return the remaining sheets to their polythene bag at once, pressing out the air before closing.

Serves 6

340g/12oz feta cheese or a crumbly goat's cheese
pepper
pinch of nutmeg
1 good bunch mint, parsley or dill, finely chopped
225g/8oz filo pastry
3–4 tbsp melted butter or oil

To make the filling, mash the cheese with a fork and mix in pepper, nutmeg and the herbs. Cut the pastry sheets with scissors into rectangular strips about 7.5cm/3in wide and put them in a pile so that those underneath do not dry out (they can do so very quickly if they are not kept covered).

Brush the top of one strip very lightly with butter or oil. Put a heaped tsp of filling at one end and roll up the pastry lengthways over it. Turn the ends in about a third of the way along to trap the filling, then continue to roll like a cigarette, leaving the ends seemingly open. Do the same with the rest of the pastry and place all the little rolls on a greased baking sheet. Brush the tops very lightly with butter or oil. Bake in a moderate oven, 180°C/350°F/gas mark 4, for about 25 minutes or until golden.

CLAUDIA RODEN

Simone Sekers writes: FILO PASTRY is paper-thin pastry sheets made with flour and water. They can enclose any number of different fillings, and are popular as a lighter alternative to the usual kinds of pastry. Widely stocked by supermarkets and delicatessens (look for it in freezer cabinets) containing 12 large sheets, it should be frozen if not used straight away, but not kept for too long as it can dry out. It can be refrozen (wrapped in convenient amounts very thoroughly in plenty of foil to help keep it supple) if you use only half the amount, as in this recipe.

Chinese cabbage, walnut and sharon fruit salad ⓥ

This salad strikes the right seasonal note, and provides a light start to a festive meal. Sharon fruit (which are imported from Israel but originate from China) look like a waxy, orange beef tomato and are widely available around Christmas time. They should be eaten when soft and ripe.

Serves 4

170–225g/6–8oz Chinese cabbage
1–2 tbsp chopped walnuts, plus 2 tbsp walnut oil
salt (optional)
2 soft, ripe sharon fruit
3 fresh dates, each stoned and sliced into 8 slivers
watercress or salad leaves for garnish

Slice the Chinese cabbage leaves lengthwise, then shred crosswise finely. Toss with the walnuts and walnut oil, seasoning with a pinch of salt if liked, and divide between 4 plates. Cut each sharon fruit in half, slicing each half into 4 segments. Arrange prettily in a star shape on top of the salad, with slivers of fresh date in between. Tuck the watercress or other leaves around the edge and serve as a first course. A little of the watercress can be chopped and tossed with the Chinese cabbage.

LYNDA BROWN

Cranberry wholewheat muffins

Makes 12-18

110g/4oz butter
110g/4oz caster sugar
2 large eggs
240ml/8fl. oz milk
110g/4oz plain flour
110g/4oz wholemeal flour
1 tbsp baking powder
55g/2oz chopped walnuts
110g/4oz cranberries

Cream the butter and sugar together and beat in the eggs. Add the milk and then the flours, baking powder, nuts and berries. Mix until the ingredients are moistened: do not beat. Put the mixture into 12–18 deep mince pie or bun tins lined with paper cases, filling them to the top. Bake in a preheated moderate oven, 180°C/350°F/gas mark 4, for 30–35 minutes until well risen and golden brown. Serve warm with butter.

THANE PRINCE

Simone Sekers writes: CRANBERRIES, native to North America and almost synonymous with turkey at Thanksgiving there, are tart red berries which come from the same family as the much milder blueberry and our own bilberry. Available here from late autumn until well beyond Christmas, they are usually sold in packs. Check each pack before you buy for any soft or shrivelled berries. Once bought they will keep well in the refrigerator, partly because of their own inherent benzoic acid content which acts as a natural preservative.

Chestnut soup

Along with Brussels sprouts, chestnuts are the traditional partner to roast turkey, and a real seasonal treat. They also make ambrosial soups. This is one of the simplest you will find, and it freezes well. It makes a good first course before the festive roast goose (p. 224–5), pheasant, or saddle of venison (p. 84). (For other suitable recipes and notes on buying and preparing chestnuts, see p. 96.)

Serves 4

225g/8oz cooked chestnut flesh
450ml/15fl. oz each beef or game stock and water; or
use 850ml/1½ pt vegetable stock
1 large stick celery
extra water if necessary, plus a little cream or creamy
milk to finish

Simmer the first three ingredients in an uncovered pan for 30 minutes. Remove the celery and blend until smooth. Adjust the consistency to that of thin cream with water plus cream or creamy milk to taste, and serve.

LYNDA BROWN

Braised red cabbage ⓥ

Serves 6–8

675g/1½ lb red cabbage
1 small onion, chopped
30g/1oz butter
1 clove garlic, crushed
2 cooking apples, peeled and chopped
1 tbsp wine vinegar
2 tbsp brown sugar

Slice the red cabbage. Fry the onion in the butter in an ovenproof casserole until soft, add the garlic and cook for a further 2–3 minutes. Stir in the rest of the ingredients, cover, and either simmer over a low heat or bake in a moderate oven, 180°C/350°F/gas mark 4, for 1½ hours, stirring occasionally. Serve with roast goose, venison or game.

THANE PRINCE

Roast goose with peach and veal stuffing

Traditional roast goose is a perfect choice for a Christmas feast and the ideal meat to have with all the fruity Christmas accompaniments and side dishes.

There are a few things to bear in mind. It *is* a very fatty bird, but this is good news as a properly cooked goose is not only moist but gives you pints of fat to use in later cooking. With a little care you can cook the stuffing inside the bird without it being too rich to eat. As goose has a relatively small amount of meat, it is a good idea to supplement this with a meat stuffing.

Always cook goose on a rack over a deep pan, or directly on the oven shelf with a large dish to catch the fat underneath, to ensure that the skin is crisp all over. Before roasting, prick the goose to allow the fat to run out as it cooks, and rub it well with salt.

Goose is best well roasted, uncovered, and, as the fat will baste the meat as it cooks, there is no need to turn the bird on to its breast. The goose liver will make a creditable pâté should you choose not to include it in the stuffing: make it on Christmas Eve to serve spread on toast with drinks before lunch.

THANE PRINCE

Serves 8

1 4.5–5.5kg/10–12lb goose with giblets

For the stuffing
110g/4oz dried peaches, soaked overnight
1 onion, finely chopped
1 tbsp olive oil
55g/2oz pine nuts
450g/1lb minced veal
110g/4oz fresh breadcrumbs
1 egg, beaten
1 bunch fresh sage, chopped
juice and grated rind of 1 small scrubbed lemon
salt and pepper

potatoes for roasting

To make the stuffing, chop the peaches and reserve. Fry the onion in the olive oil until golden, then add the pine nuts and fry briefly, stirring, until coloured. Remove from the heat and combine all the remaining ingredients thoroughly.

Remove all the visible internal fat from the goose and stuff the cavity. Truss the goose lightly and prick the skin all over with a sharp fork (do not tear the skin or prick deeply into the flesh), then rub with salt.

Put the goose on a rack or trivet over a deep pan into a preheated hot oven, 220°C/425°F/gas mark 7, and cook for 1 hour. Pour off the fat that has collected and turn the oven down to 180°C/350°F/gas mark 4. Continue to cook for a further 1½ hours. Turn up the oven to 220°C/425°F/ gas mark 7 to crisp the skin and cook for a final 30–40 minutes. Test by piercing the leg of the goose to see if the juices run clear. Allow the goose to rest for at least 15 minutes before carving.

To roast the potatoes to accompany the goose, drain off most of the fat which has collected in the pan under the goose 1½ hours before the end of the cooking time and put some parboiled potatoes into the pan. The fat will drip over them to baste them.

Boil the giblets in water with appropriate seasonings to make a concentrated stock, and use this to make a gravy in the usual way.

THANE PRINCE

Simone Sekers writes: GOOSE resists all attempts to farm it intensively, and for this reason is still a purely seasonal treat from Michaelmas (when it was traditionally eaten in the Midlands) until Christmas. Rich dark flesh and copious amounts of fat on a heavy framework of bones means that, like duck, a large goose feeds fewer people than you think. A bird

225

weighing about 4.5kg/10lb, oven-ready, will provide 2 helpings each for about 8 people. Always keep any fat left over from the cooking as it makes superlative roast potatoes.

Duck with pears

This is a festive Spanish dish from Claudia Roden. The *picada*, a fragrant mixture of almonds and garlic used to flavour and thicken the broth, is a famous Catalan sauce.

Serves 6

1 duck weighing about 2.25kg/5lb, cut into 6 pieces; or
use 6 breasts or legs
2 tbsp olive oil
6 unripe pears
1 cinnamon stick

For the sauce
2 medium onions, sliced
1 medium carrot, sliced
2 medium ripe tomatoes, peeled, de-seeded and
chopped
3 tbsp olive oil
300ml/10fl. oz meat or chicken stock or water
120ml/4fl. oz Spanish brandy
pinch of dried thyme
salt

For the picada
3–4 cloves garlic
55g/2oz blanched almonds, toasted

Brown the duck pieces evenly in the olive oil in a frying pan, for about 10–15 minutes. The duck will lose quite a lot of fat, which should be discarded. Meanwhile, cover the pears in water and boil with the cinnamon stick for about 20 minutes or until tender; do not let them fall apart. Drain and reserve the cooking liquid.

To make the sauce, soften the onions, carrot and tomatoes in the olive oil. Add the stock or water, brandy, thyme and salt, plus about the same quantity of cooking liquid from the pears, and simmer for 30 minutes. Transfer to a blender or food processor and blend until smooth. Return the sauce to the pan, add the duck and cook gently for about 45 minutes or until the duck is tender.

To make the *picada*, pound the garlic and almonds to a paste with a pestle and mortar, or use a blender or food processor. Stir this mixture into the duck sauce and cook for 10 minutes longer. Serve the duck pieces with the sauce poured over, and decorate with warmed pear halves.

CLAUDIA RODEN

Salmon with an orange mousseline, watercress and orange sauce

Serves 6

900g/2lb salmon

For the stock
celery
carrot
onion
bay leaf
1 sprig dried thyme
6 peppercorns

For the mousseline
340g/12oz whiting fillet or haddock, skinned and
boned
240ml/8fl. oz double cream
2 egg whites
grated rind 1/2 small scrubbed orange
1/4 tsp each freshly ground coriander and allspice
salt and pepper

For the sauce
leaves from small bunch watercress
300ml/10fl. oz strong fish stock
juice 1 orange
150ml/5fl. oz single cream
1 tsp cornflour
salt and pepper

watercress leaves and thinly sliced orange to garnish
(optional)

Ask the fishmonger for a whole piece of salmon from the centre of the fish and ask him to fillet and skin it. From the trimmings, plus any extra (use the trimmings from the whiting or haddock), make a strong fish stock with the chopped vegetables and seasonings, with enough water to cover. Simmer for 20–30 minutes, strain, then reduce to just over 300ml/10fl. oz and reserve.

Next, make the mousseline. Cut the whiting or haddock into chunks and chill, together with the food processor bowl and the cream by putting them all in the freezer for about 20 minutes. Blend the fish to the finest paste you can achieve, then add the egg whites, one by one, with the motor running. Add the grated orange rind, coriander and allspice, then check to see that the fish mixture is still very cold. If not, put it back into the freezer for 10 minutes. When cold, add the cream slowly through the funnel. Season with salt and pepper to taste.

Season both salmon fillets lightly, then sandwich them together with the mousseline. Butter a generous piece of foil, place the salmon in the centre, add 1–2 tbsp of fish stock and fold the edges of the foil together tightly to enclose the fish. All this can be done in advance and the prepared fish kept in the fridge. Bake the fish parcel for 50 minutes in a preheated oven, 160°C/325°F/gas mark 3. When it is done (the fish will flake easily), slide it on to a serving dish and keep warm, covered with foil.

The sauce can be made while the fish is cooking and kept warm over a pan of simmering water. Put the watercress leaves and fish stock into the processor and purée, then add orange juice to taste – the orange flavour shouldn't predominate. Mix the cream with the cornflour and add to the processor, then transfer the mixture to a saucepan. Stir over a low heat until the sauce thickens a little and the flavours blend. Season to taste. Garnish the salmon with more watercress and thinly sliced orange if you like, and serve the sauce separately. Alternatively, flood each plate with the sauce and serve a slice of salmon on its side to show off the pink and orange colours.

SIMONE SEKERS

FESTIVE FILO PASTRIES

CATERING for a vegetarian member of the family at Christmas is becoming commonplace and doesn't necessarily have to involve two separate dinners. The following savoury crisp filo pastries are designed merely to replace the turkey.

The fillings can all be prepared in advance, leaving just the final assembly which can be timed with the rest of the dinner quite easily. These quantities are for single servings, but can be increased as necessary. For ease, I use Yorkshire pudding tins to cook them in, but they can be fashioned into any shape or size you like, including a jaunty Christmas cracker shape which can be managed without too much difficulty. Allow two or three per person, each with a different filling.

Wild rice, mushroom and garlic filo pastries

Serves 1

1 dsp (7g/¹/₄oz) each of wild rice and
white basmati rice
7g/¹/₄oz dried wild mushrooms (ceps or morels),
roughly chopped
30g/1oz fresh mushrooms
¹/₂ clove chopped garlic
¹/₂ small onion
7g/¹/₄ oz butter
salt

Cover the wild rice with water and cook for 10 minutes in a small covered pan. Add the white rice and dried mushrooms, re-cover and cook for a further 5 minutes. Leave to cool in the pan, keeping the lid on. Meanwhile, process the fresh mushrooms, garlic and onion to a paste in a food processor. Soften in a little butter for 3–4 minutes; the paste should still be wet. Drain off any excess moisture from the rice. Lightly mix everything together, season with salt, and proceed as below.

Brazil nut, lemon and celery filo pastries

Serves 1

45g/1½ oz brazil nuts
45g/1½ oz prepared celery, cut into tiny dice
7g/¼oz butter
1tsp raisins
1 tbsp cream
a little finely grated scrubbed lemon rind

Process the nuts to a gritty paste in the food processor. Soften the celery for 3–4 minutes in a little butter. Cool. Lightly mix everything together, adding lemon rind to taste. Proceed as below.

Savoury leek and Brie filo pastries

Serves 1

45g/1½oz de-rinded Brie
45g/1½oz prepared leeks, finely chopped
¼ tsp finely chopped tarragon or rosemary (optional)

Dice the Brie into large chunks and leave in the freezer for 1 hour to harden – this prevents it from melting too quickly in the oven. Soften the leeks in a little butter for 5 minutes. Cool. Stir in herbs if using, add the Brie just before baking, and proceed as below.

To assemble the pastries, fold a single sheet of filo (*see* p. 221) in half, then cut into quarters. This gives you 4 small squares, each of double thickness. Place one square in a greased Yorkshire pudding tin (mine has holes for four individual puddings), or something similar. Brush the edges with olive oil or melted butter and pile the filling into the centre. Arrange a second square on top, giving it a half turn so the pastry has 8 corners. Brush the top lightly with oil or butter. Tuck well down around the filling, leaving the pointed ends sticking up like a frill. With luck you should end up with something approaching a sunflower. Bake immediately in a very hot oven, 220°C/425°F/gas mark 7, for 10 minutes until golden brown. Ease out with a palette knife and serve immediately.

LYNDA BROWN

Simone Sekers writes: WILD RICE is the grain of a North American aquatic grass, rather than a true rice, and is extremely nutritious and somewhat expensive. Because of its last two qualities, it can be combined with other long-grain rices using 55g/2oz wild rice per 225g/8oz of brown or white rice (basmati is best), where it will impart its exotic flavour. It is also very good with game. Now available in most supermarkets, it is sometimes sold already mixed with ordinary rice.

LEFTOVERS

'Leftovers' is one of the most dismal words I can think of in the English language, and too often is used to describe what can actually be very good to eat and most satisfying to make. Here are a few worthy ideas, beginning with two delectable dishes for turkey from Simone Sekers.

Turkey with four cheeses

'This recipe is one for which I will actually create leftovers of a turkey or chicken,' writes Simone Sekers. 'It is based on the Italian *Quattro Formaggi* sauce, but uses four British cheeses instead. You can vary the combination to suit yourself, but I advise one strong cheese, one blue cheese, one 'herb' cheese and one soft, bland cheese to get the balance right.'

Serves 4

340g/12oz diced cooked turkey
85g/3oz each of mature Cheddar, Stilton, Sage Derby or
Lancashire, and Single Gloucester
600ml/1 pt milk
55g/2oz each of butter and flour
bay leaf
salt, pepper and nutmeg

Start by making a béchamel sauce with the butter, flour and milk, and leave it to simmer with the bay leaf in it while you prepare the cheeses.

Grate the Cheddar, crumble the Stilton, cube the Sage Derby or Lancashire, and cut the Single Gloucester into thin strips. When the béchamel is well flavoured and creamy, remove the bay leaf and season the sauce with a little salt (the cheeses will add more saltiness), freshly ground pepper and nutmeg.

Stir in the turkey and continue to simmer until the turkey is really hot – about 10–15 minutes. Take the pan off the heat, then add the Cheddar first, stirring well. When it has melted, fold in the other cheeses lightly so that they don't break up too much, and serve at once.

You can serve this either as a sauce for pasta or with boiled Italian rice, or you can add 100g/3½ oz cooked pasta to it and brown the whole dish under the grill, with more grated Cheddar on top.

SIMONE SEKERS

Pulled and devilled turkey
(or chicken, or pheasant)

Serves 4

approx. 450g/1lb cooked dark meat from the legs and
wings, in largish pieces
340g/12oz cooked breast meat

For the devil sauce
3 tbsp sunflower oil
1 tbsp soy sauce
1 tbsp Worcester sauce
3 tbsp mango or tomato chutney
a few drops of Tabasco
salt and plenty of freshly ground black pepper

For the cream sauce
300ml/10fl. oz double cream
150ml/5fl. oz single cream
salt, pepper and squeeze lemon juice

Mix together all the ingredients for the devil sauce and use it to coat the
dark meat pieces thoroughly. Leave to marinate for as long as possible,
but at least 1 hour. Meanwhile, pull the breast meat into fibrous pieces
that follow the grain of the meat, but don't make them too fine.

Arrange the devilled meat in a shallow dish in one layer and cook
under a hot grill until the meat begins to crisp and the marinade to bubble. While you do this, heat the two creams in a frying pan over a
medium heat, and when it comes to the boil, add the breast meat. Lower
the heat and leave to heat through, then season with salt, pepper and
lemon juice. Arrange the devilled meat on a shallow platter, with the
pulled meat in the centre. Serve with plain boiled basmati rice and a
salad.

SIMONE SEKERS

Jambalaya

This is a Cajun dish from the American South.

Serves 4–5

450g/1lb diced cooked ham
1 large onion, chopped
2 tbsp olive oil
1–2 cloves crushed garlic
1 stick celery, chopped
1 green pepper, chopped
225g/8oz rice, preferably risotto type (arborio)
400g/14oz tinned tomatoes, chopped
1–2 tbsp tomato purée (optional)
$1/2$ tsp crushed thyme
$1/8$ tsp cayenne pepper, or to taste
salt and pepper
approx. 600ml/1pt chicken or ham stock

To finish
55–110g/2–4 oz defrosted prawns
2 tbsp chopped parsley

Fry the onion in the olive oil in a casserole or heavy saucepan until soft and transparent. Add the garlic, celery and green pepper and fry for 3–4 minutes, stirring. Add the rice and stir-fry for a further 2–3 minutes until it has been coated with oil, then add the ham, chopped tomatoes, tomato purée if using, thyme, cayenne, black pepper and about 450ml/15fl. oz stock. Stir well, adding a little salt if needed.

Cover the rice and simmer, stirring occasionally and adding extra stock as needed. When the rice is cooked, stir in the prawns and heat through, add the chopped parsley and serve.

THANE PRINCE

Stilton beignets Ⓥ

Serves 6

For the choux pastry
scant 240ml/8fl. oz water
85g/3oz butter
110g/4oz plain flour
3 eggs, beaten

170g/6oz Stilton trimmings
45g/1½oz grated Parmesan cheese (*see* p. 197)
½ tsp paprika
salt and pepper to taste
vegetable oil for deep-frying

First make a choux pastry dough: put the water and butter in a saucepan and heat to melt the butter. Bring to the boil and remove from the heat. Add all the flour immediately, beating vigorously with a wooden spoon. The smooth dough will collect in a ball in the saucepan. Allow this to cool for 5 minutes, then beat in the eggs a little at a time; the mixture will gradually become soft and glossy. When all the egg has been added, stir in the 2 cheeses, paprika and seasoning and mix thoroughly.

Heat the oil in a deep-fat frying pan, and when it is hot (check by frying a cube of bread; it should crisp and brown in 60 seconds), carefully drop spoonfuls of the mixture into the pan. Cook the *beignets* a few at a time for about 4 minutes, turning occasionally. When each batch is done, place them in an ovenproof dish on crumpled kitchen paper and keep them warm in a hot oven while you finish cooking.

Leftover cranberry sauce goes well with these. Add the juice of an orange, bring it to the boil and serve with the *beignets*.   THANE PRINCE

Editor's note: Leftover cranberry sauce makes an admirable filling for turkey sandwiches, but is excellent used in other ways – with grilled or fried plaice or other white fish, for example, with the Stilton *beignets* above, or as a stuffing for pheasant by mixing half a chopped apple with the same amount of leftover cranberry sauce, a chopped stalk of celery softened in butter, and a couple of tablespoons of undercooked brown rice.

Cranberry sauce is also excellent with individual portions of deep-fried Camembert cheese. Coat with beaten egg and breadcrumbs twice, and just before you want them put them in the freezer for 10 minutes to chill. Deep-fry as above for 2–3 minutes until brown. Serve immediately with slices of thin, dark rye bread.

Oriental dried fruit and nut sweetmeats

These elegant little sweetmeats from Claudia Roden are a charming way of using up the dried fruit and nuts which are usually left over at Christmas. Children could probably be happily entrusted to roll out and shape them.

Apricot drops: Process 225g/8oz of the sharp, brownish apricots to a stiff paste in a food processor, aided by a little water added 1 tbsp at a time, plus 2 tbsp of icing sugar, or to taste. Shape into small balls, roll in icing sugar and stick half a pistachio nut on top of each one.

Date drops: Process 225g/8oz dried pitted dates (the kind you get in a solid block) to a stiff paste in a food processor, with 1 tsp cinnamon, 1/2 tsp ground cardamom and a little water added 1 tbsp at a time. Scrape out and, using your hands, work in 100g/3¹/₂oz coarsely chopped walnuts. Shape into little balls and roll in icing sugar.

Stuffed dates: For the filling, mix 170g/6oz ground almonds with 85g/3oz caster sugar to a paste with 2–4 tbsp of rose- or orange-flower water. Using 450g/1lb dried dates (the moist boxed California type), make a slit in one side of each and pull out the stone. Press in a small sausage-shaped lump of almond paste and close the date slightly.

CLAUDIA RODEN

236

DESSERTS AND CAKES

Sicilian cheesecake

This party dish, a speciality of Palermo, is extremely rich and a little goes a long way, writes Claudia Roden.

Serves 20

1kg/2¼ lb ricotta cheese (*see* p. 210)
100g/2½ oz icing sugar, or to taste
4 drops vanilla essence, or 1 tsp grated orange or
lemon zest
100g/3½ oz bitter chocolate, grated
285g/10oz mixed candied fruit, including if possible
pumpkin and orange peel, chopped small
285g/10oz sponge fingers or slices of sponge cake
170ml/6fl.oz rum, or to taste

Beat the ricotta with about 70g/2½oz of the sugar and the vanilla or zest, then fold in the chocolate and candied fruit, reserving a few tablespoons to decorate the top of the cake.

Line a 25cm/10in cake tin or mould with greaseproof paper or kitchen foil so that you can turn the cake out easily. Dip the sponge fingers or cake in rum for a few seconds, just enough to moisten and soften them slightly, and use them to line the bottom and sides of the tin or mould. Spread the ricotta mixture evenly inside and cover with the rest of the sponge fingers or slices dipped in rum. Cover with a piece of foil and press down hard. Refrigerate for at least 1 hour until firm. To serve, remove the cover, turn the cake upside down and remove the rest of the lining. Sprinkle the cake with icing sugar and decorate with the remaining chopped fruit.

CLAUDIA RODEN

Betty Allen's Atholl Brose

Atholl Brose is the famous Highland drink of oatmeal, whisky and honey, with which Scots traditionally toast the New Year. Here it is adapted into a delectable instant dessert. Be careful not to overbeat the cream; the final mixture should be floppy not stiff.

Serves 4

30g/1oz medium oatmeal
2 tbsp malt whisky
2 tbsp clear honey
300ml/10fl. oz double cream

Toast the oatmeal under the grill and leave to cool. Stir the whisky into the honey. Lightly whisk the cream until it *just* begins to thicken. Fold in the other ingredients, pile into decorative glasses and chill for 2 hours. (The mixture will stiffen somewhat.) Leave at room temperature for 15 minutes before serving.

For a lighter version, which is also very good, the double cream may be substituted with the rich Greek-style yoghurt, or with a mixture of cream and ordinary yoghurt. Beat it first and proceed as above.

LYNDA BROWN

Medieval rice pudding with honey and almonds

This is a delicious variation on the old favourite, served in individual ramekin dishes.

Serves 4

55g/2oz pudding rice
55g/2oz ground almonds; or 45g/1¹/₂oz chopped almonds, toasted light brown
600ml/1pt milk
1 tsp cinnamon or 2–3 pinches powdered saffron (*see* p. 69)
4 tsp clear runny honey, plus extra to serve

Put the rice into a pan of water and boil for 5 minutes. Drain and divide between 4 ramekin dishes measuring 9cm/3¹/₂in across. Mix in the almonds. Bring the milk to the boil, adding the cinnamon or sufficient saffron to colour the milk yellow, and fill each ramekin dish. Bake in a low oven, 140°C/275°F/gas mark 1, for 1–1¼ hours until the milk has been almost absorbed and the rice is soft and creamy. Cool for 5 minutes. Spread 1 tsp of clear honey over the surface of each dish, and serve with extra honey for people to help themselves.

LYNDA BROWN

Twelfth Day strudel

Serves 6–8

4 sheets filo pastry (see p. 221)

For the filling
approx. 30–45g/1–1½ oz melted butter for brushing the
filo
340g/12oz eating apples, weighed after peeling
and coring
170g/6oz mincemeat
30g/1oz toasted hazelnuts, skins rubbed off and
coarsely chopped
30g/1oz ground almonds
½ tsp cinnamon
3–4 tbsp rum or brandy
30g/1oz brown breadcrumbs, toasted
1–2 tbsp soft brown sugar (optional)
1 tsp rosewater (optional)

Grease a baking sheet with some of the melted butter. Spread the sheets of filo on top of each other on the baking sheet, lightly brushing each with a little melted butter. Slice the apples thinly (this can be done in a food processor). Mix lightly with all the other ingredients, adding the soft brown sugar and rosewater if liked. Heap up the mixture on the filo pastry down the length of the centre. Fold over the two sides and join the ends. Brush with the remaining melted butter, sealing the join, and make small cuts down the centre. Bake at 190°C/375°F/gas mark 5 for 35–40 minutes until well browned. Serve warm or at room temperature, but not straight from the refrigerator.

LYNDA BROWN

Prune, almond and brandy tart

Serves 6–8

225g/8oz prunes in brandy (*see* below)
23cm/9in unbaked shortcrust pie shell (allow 225g/8oz
shortcrust pastry)
300ml/10fl. oz sour cream
3 egg yolks
55g/2oz caster sugar
55g/2oz ground almonds
45g/1½ oz melted butter
1–2 tbsp brandy

Drain and stone the prunes and arrange on the uncooked piecrust. Beat all the remaining ingredients together well and pour over the prunes. Bake in a preheated oven, 190°C/375°F/gas mark 5, for 30–40 minutes until golden brown. Serve warm. This may be made ahead and reheated.

THANE PRINCE

Quick prunes in brandy

225g/8oz dried prunes, washed well in hot water
cold tea to cover
1 tbsp brown sugar
approx. 150ml/5fl. oz brandy

Cover the prunes with tea and soak overnight. Add the sugar, bring to the boil and simmer gently for 2–3 minutes. Drain and put the prunes in a deep jar (a Kilner jar is ideal), cover with brandy, adding 2–3 tbsp of the juice left in the pan, and seal the jar. They may be used after 2–3 days, or left until required and will keep for many years.

THANE PRINCE

Galette du rois, King's cake

French and Spanish bakers make this cake, a kind of shortbread, through-out January as a traditional part of the festivities. It is customary to hide a dried bean in the cake – whoever finds it becomes the king or queen and rules for the day, a tradition which dates back many centuries. (Until the middle of the nineteenth century the splendidly decorated Twelfth Day cake, eaten on 6 January, performed the same role in this country and was an important part of Christmas celebrations.) The usual size for a *Galette du rois* is about 35cm/14in across. This is for a smaller one, about half that size, but you can double the quantities if you like.

It is best eaten while still warm – and don't forget to tell everyone about the bean, a sign of good luck for the coming year.

Serves 4–6

125g/4½oz plain flour
100g/3½oz unsalted butter
scant ½ level tsp salt
1 level tsp sugar
2 tbsp plus 1 dsp water (approx. 40ml/1¼ fl. oz)
a little beaten egg yolk for glazing
extra flour for dusting

Sift the flour into a bowl, make a well in the centre and put in the butter. Dissolve the salt and sugar in the water and pour into the well. Using a fork at first, then your fingers, roughly mix the butter and water, gradually incorporating the flour until a firmish dough is formed. Do not knead. Gather the dough into a ball, flour lightly, wrap, and let the dough rest in a cool place for 45 minutes.

On a floured surface, roll out the dough into a rectangle, 45 x 15cm/ 18 x 6in. Fold in thirds (to make a square) and let it rest for 10 minutes. Repeat this process twice more, always rolling and folding in the opposite direction. After the third time, bring the corners over the dough, pressing down firmly with your fingertips. Now bring over the edges between the corners in the same way, thus fashioning the dough into a round. Using your fingers and rolling pin, shape the dough into a smooth circle 7mm–1.25cm /¼–½in thick (no thicker or it will not cook through in the centre properly) and about 17.5cm/7in across.

Press a dried bean into the dough and turn it over, bringing the smoothest side to the top. Using a sharp knife, score around the edge from top to bottom, and notch the rim to give a scalloped effect as you would a pie. Place on an ungreased baking sheet. Brush the top with egg glaze, taking care not to let it drip over on to the edge. Finally, score the surface deeply with a criss-cross or lattice design and prick all over with a fork, again deep into the pastry.

Bake for 40–45 minutes in a preheated hot oven, 200°C/400°F/gas mark 6, until golden brown and cooked through.

LYNDA BROWN

INDEX

The Daily Telegraph

Weekend
Cookbook